Pattern-based Approaches to NLP in the Age of Deep Learning (PAN-DL 2022)

Gyeongju, South Korea
12-17 October 2022

ISBN: 978-1-7138-6193-5

Printed from e-media with permission by:

Curran Associates, Inc.
57 Morehouse Lane
Red Hook, NY 12571

Some format issues inherent in the e-media version may also appear in this print version.

Printed with permission by Curran Associates, Inc. (2023)

For permission requests, please contact the Association for Computational Linguistics at the address below.

Association for Computational Linguistics
209 N. Eighth Street
Stroudsburg, Pennsylvania 18360

Phone: 1-570-476-8006
Fax: 1-570-476-0860

acl@aclweb.org

Additional copies of this publication are available from:

Curran Associates, Inc.
57 Morehouse Lane
Red Hook, NY 12571 USA
Phone: 845-758-0400
Fax: 845-758-2633
Email: curran@proceedings.com
Web: www.proceedings.com

COLING

International Conference on Computational Linguistics

Proceedings of the Conference and Workshops

COLING

Volume 29 (2022), No. 5

Proceedings of Pattern-based Approaches to NLP in the Age of Deep Learning (PAN-DL)

The 29th International Conference on Computational Linguistics

October 12 - 17, 2022
Gyeongju, Republic of Korea

Message from the Organizers

Welcome to the first edition of the Workshop on Pattern-based Approaches to NLP in the Age of Deep Learning (Pan-DL)! Our workshop is being organized online on October 17, 2022, in conjunction with the 29th International Conference on Computational Linguistics (COLING).

We all know that deep-learning methods have dominated the field of natural language processing in the past decade. However, these approaches usually rely on the availability of high-quality and high-quantity data annotation. Furthermore, the learned models are difficult to interpret and incur substantial technical debt. As a result, these approaches tend to exclude users that lack the necessary machine learning background. In contrast, rule-based methods are easier to deploy and adapt; they support human examination of intermediate representations and reasoning steps; they are more transparent to subject-matter experts; they are amenable to having a human in the loop through intervention, manipulation and incorporation of domain knowledge; and further the resulting systems tend to be lightweight and fast. This workshop focuses on all aspects of rule-based approaches, including their application, representation, and interpretability, as well as their strengths and weaknesses relative to state-of-the-art machine learning approaches.

Considering the large number of potential directions in this neuro-symbolic space, we emphasized inclusivity in our workshop. We received 13 papers and accepted 10 for oral presentation. This resulted in an overall acceptance rate of 77%.

In addition of the oral presentations of the accepted papers, our workshop includes a keynote talk by Ellen Riloff, who has made crucial contributions to the field of natural language processing, many of which are at the intersection of rule- and neural-based methods. Further, the workshop contains a panel that will discuss the merits and limitations of rules in our neural era. The panelists will be academics with expertise in both neural- and rule-based methods, industry experts that employ these methods for commercial products, government officials in charge of AI funding, organizers of natural language processing evaluations, and subject matter experts that have used rule-based methods for domain-specific applications.

We thank Ellen Riloff and the panelists for their important contribution to our workshop!

Finally, we are thankful to the members of the program committee for their insightful reviews! We are confident that all submissions have benefited from their expert feedback. Their contribution was a key factor for accepting a diverse and high-quality list of papers, which we hope will make the first edition of the Pan-DL workshop a success, and will motivate many future editions.

Pan-DL 2022 Organizers
October 2022

Organizing Committee:

Laura Chiticariu, IBM, USA
Yoav Goldberg, Bar Ilan University, Israel
Gus Hahn-Powell, University of Arizona, USA
Clayton T. Morrison, University of Arizona, USA
Rebecca Sharp, Lex Machina, USA
Mihai Surdeanu, University of Arizona, USA
Marco Valenzuela-Escárcega, University of Arizona, USA
Enrique Noriega-Atala, University of Arizona, USA
Aakanksha Naik, Carnegie Mellon University, USA

Program Committee:

Dane Bell, The RiverStone Group, USA
Maria Alexeeva, University of Arizona, USA
Xuan Wang, University of Illinois at Urbana-Champaign, USA
Daniela Claro, Universidade Federal da Bahia, Brazil
Anthony Rios, University of Texas at San Antonio, USA
Aryeh Tiktinsky, Allen Institute for AI (AI2), USA
Juan Diego Rodriguez, University of Texas at Austin, USA
Hillel Taub-Tabib, Allen Institute for AI (AI2), Israel
Roberty Vavareanu, University of Arizona, USA
Andrew Zupon, Google, USA
Hoang N.H Van, University of Arizona, USA

Table of Contents

PatternRank: Jointly Ranking Patterns and Extractions for Relation Extraction Using Graph-Based Algorithms

Robert Vacareanu♠,♣, Dane Bell*, and Mihai Surdeanu♠

♠University of Arizona, Tucson, AZ, USA
*LUM.ai, Tucson, AZ, USA
♣Technical University of Cluj-Napoca, Cluj-Napoca, Romania
{rvacareanu,msurdeanu}@arizona.edu, dane@lum.ai

Abstract

In this paper we revisit the direction of using lexico-syntactic patterns for relation extraction instead of today's ubiquitous neural classifiers. We propose a semi-supervised graph-based algorithm for pattern acquisition that scores patterns and the relations they extract jointly, using a variant of PageRank (Page et al., 1999). We insert light supervision in the form of seed patterns or relations, and model it with several custom teleportation probabilities that bias random-walk scores of patterns/relations based on their proximity to correct information. We evaluate our approach on Few-Shot TACRED (Zhang et al., 2017; Sabo et al., 2021), and show that our method outperforms (or performs competitively with) more expensive and opaque deep neural networks. Lastly, we thoroughly compare our proposed approach with the seminal RlogF pattern acquisition algorithm of Riloff (1996), showing that it outperforms it for all the hyper parameters tested, in all settings.[1]

1 Introduction

Rule-based methods hastily fell out of favor after the "deep learning tsunami" hit natural language processing (Manning, 2015). However, deep learning methods are not perfect: they continue to remain "blackboxes," despite recent effort towards untangling their representations (Jain and Wallace, 2019; Wiegreffe and Pinter, 2019; Kobayashi et al., 2020). Moreover, the presence of various linguistic phenomenons in the hidden representation of deep models does not imply that the model will use them (McCoy et al., 2019). On the other hand, rules are interpretable by design. Furthermore, changing something in a deep learning model often changes everything (Sculley et al., 2015; Arpteg et al., 2018), while rules are disentangled, i.e., modifying a rule impacts only its own matches.

Here, we introduce a novel pattern acquisition method for relation extraction, which uses graph-based techniques that operate over the entire topology of the bipartite graph that contains candidate patterns and their extracted relations. More specifically, we leverage a variant of PageRank (Page et al., 1999) to *jointly* score candidate patterns and their extractions. Such an approach has the advantage of softening the sparsity problem: an unknown, but potentially in-domain candidate relation is not automatically considered incorrect (as most "traditional" semi-supervised algorithms would consider it); instead it receives a non-zero score that depends on how reachable it is in this graph.

Our main contributions are:

- We propose a graph-based algorithm, PatternRank, for jointly scoring patterns and extractions by considering the whole topology of the graph that contains them. Our algorithm captures light supervision (in the form of seed relations or patterns) with several custom teleportation probabilities that bias random-walk scores of patterns/relations based on their proximity to correct information.

- We evaluate our proposed approach on the Few-Shot TACRED task (Zhang et al., 2017; Sabo et al., 2021). Our results show that the performance is better than (or at least equivalent with) several state-of-the-art neural approaches, while also being fully interpretable.

- We perform an extensive comparison between our proposed method and the seminal pattern acquisition algorithm RLogF of Riloff (1996), which is closest in spirit to our direction, explaining why it outperforms it.

[1] Code available at `https://github.com/clulab/releases/tree/master/pandl2022-patternrank`

Proceedings of the 29th International Conference on Computational Linguistic, pages 1–10
October 12–17, 2022.

2 Terminology

Before moving on, we introduce here key terminology used throughout the paper.

Pattern We define a *pattern* as a linear sequence of surface and syntactic constraints. For example, the pattern `[lemma=born] >nmod_in [ne=LOC]` matches if the text contains the lemma *born*, linked through a *nmod_in* dependency to a token labeled as a *location* named entity.

Relation We evaluate our proposed method on relation classification. As such, we use the term *relation* to refer to the semantic relation holding between two given entities. For example, for the sentence `John was born in Tampa`, where the two entities are *John* and *Tampa*, respectively, the relation will be *per:born_in*.

3 Related Work

Rule-based systems received tremendous attention the "pre deep-learning era." In a seminal work, Hearst (1992) proposes a method to learn hyponymy relations using hand-written patterns of the form NP_0 `such as` $\{NP_1$ `..,` `(and|or)`$\}$ NP_n. Riloff (1993) introduced AutoSlog, a system for automatically learning domain-specific dictionaries using a few hand-written patterns. The system is improved in (Riloff, 1996) by combining the original AutoSlog with statistical techniques and introduced the RlogF pattern scoring function, defined as: $RlogF(pattern_i) = \frac{F_i}{N_i} log_2(F_i)$, where F_i is the number of extractions for the corresponding class, and N_i is the total number of extractions.

The duality between patterns and relations has also been explored in (Brin, 1998). More concretely, the authors first generate a set of patterns from a set of relations. Then, using the previously generated set of patterns they generate a new set of relations. On a high level, we employ a similar algorithm. Conceptually similar method has also been in explored in (Riloff and Jones, 1999; Riloff and Wiebe, 2003).

3.1 Automatic pattern learning

The typical approach to semi-supervised pattern learning is to initialize the learning algorithm with a small set of known seed relations (Riloff and Jones, 1999; Riloff and Wiebe, 2003; Gupta and Manning, 2014). Generally, the approach is to consider the matches outside the seed relations as incorrect matches (Riloff and Jones, 1999; Riloff and Wiebe, 2003). Gupta and Manning (2014) improved the approach by allowing soft matches. Concretely, they predict the labels on unlabeled entities using a concatenation of different features, including word embeddings. We approach this issue by interpreting the matches of all the patterns as a graph and scoring everything jointly. In a sense, our approach can be thought of as a guided wisdom of the crowd approach.

3.2 Graph-based pattern learning

Treating pattern acquisition from a graph-based perspective is an under-explored approach. However, we are not the first to view it from this point of view. Kozareva et al. (2008) briefly explored using PageRank, among other scoring techniques, but in another setting and only for relation scoring. They focused on learning hyponym relations starting from a single doubly-anchored pattern template and a single seed instance. They build a directed graph G, where an edge (u, v) represents that using the relation u in the pattern template extracted the relation v. Then, they used graph-based scoring techniques to select the best relations. In contrast, our proposed method learns both patterns and relations jointly, starting from either a pattern or a seed relation.

Perhaps the work of (Hassan et al., 2006) is closest in nature with our approach. They proposed using Hyperlink-Induced Topic Search (HITS) (Kleinberg, 1999) to jointly learn patterns and relations without any supervision. One limitation of their method is that it is unable to accommodate initial information about which seeds relations or patterns are considered correct, information which can come from a previous component in the pipeline, or from human supervision. In contrast, our algorithm can incorporate human supervision through seed relations or patterns, and we use a new topic-sensitive variant of PageRank (Page et al., 1999) to model human supervision during the random walk.

Although rule-based approaches received a lot of attention prior to the deep-learning era, graph-based approaches for pattern acquisition remain under explored. In this paper we model the pattern scoring problem as a random walk over a graph consisting of patterns and relations, and mitigate sparsity through custom teleportation probability. We empirically show that this strategy leads to better results in realistic few-shot settings for relation extraction (Sabo et al., 2021).

4 Method

Our approach, called PatternRank, follows an iterative approach, which alternates between learning patterns from known relations (or seeds), and extracting new relations matched by these patterns. The key contribution of our work is the novel scoring strategy, which scores patterns and extracted relations jointly, using a graph-based algorithm. We describe the three components of our method in greater detail below.

4.1 Generating Candidate Patterns

We generate candidate patterns starting from a small set of seed relations and some (unannotated) text corpus. Our seed relations take the form (agent, predicate, patient), and the patterns are the syntactic paths connecting the three elements. For example, from the seed relation (*drought*, *causes*, *famine*), we consider all the syntactic paths connecting *drought* with *famine* that pass through the predicate *causes* in the corpus.[2] Then, to reduce search space, we filter these candidate patterns as follows:

1. We remove candidate patterns observed less than k times in the corpus.
2. We avoid mirror patterns. For example, if in the set of candidate patterns we have both <nsubj causes >dobj and <dobj causes >nsubj we keep the patterns that extracted more relations overall.
3. We remove patterns that contain the same type of dependencies on both sides of the predicate. For example, we filter out patterns like <nsubj causes >nsubj >dobj.

Our method accommodates the case where the starting point are seed patterns instead of seed relations. In this case we apply the seed patterns to generate seed relations. Then, we continue with pattern generation as described above.

An important difference from previous work is that our method does not use a pre-computed index with all the patterns on the corpus (Lin and Pantel, 2001). In realistic settings, such an index of rules is prohibitively large due to the sparsity of language. Instead, we generate them *on the fly* using Odinson, a rule-based information extraction framework that indexes *atomic* syntactic dependencies (Valenzuela-Escárcega et al., 2020). To bridge the fact that the Odinson index contains individual syntactic dependencies, whereas our rules are compositional (i.e. they aggregate multiple atomic (word- or dependency-level) constraints such as matching lemmas or part-of-speech tags), we create patterns by searching the Odinson for all the syntactic paths connecting the seed relations. For example, for the seed relation (*drought*, *causes*, *famine*) we search for the paths connecting *drought* to *famine* via *causes* with the Odinson query: [lemma=drought] («|»)* [lemma=cause] («|»)* [lemma=famine], where («|»)* stands for zero or more syntactic dependencies connecting the token to the left to the one on the right. This significantly speeds up pattern generation without relying on an explicit pattern index.

4.2 Extracting Candidate Relations

Using the previously generated patterns, we apply them over our corpora and record the relations matched by them. We filter the extractions based on the part-of-speech tags of the constituent words and based on their concreteness. For example, we remove relations where the agent or patient are pronouns or symbols. Further, we use the concreteness norm database of Brysbaert et al. (2014)[3] to filter out relations that are too generic (e.g., (someone, causes, something)). The threshold is an application specific hyper parameter.

4.3 Scoring Patterns and Relations

We score patterns and relations jointly using a graph-based algorithm. Specifically, we view the patterns and relations as a bipartite graph. Nodes represent patterns or relations. Edges between nodes of the same type are prohibited. Two nodes are connected with an edge if the corresponding pattern matched the corresponding relation. Edges are undirected, as the pattern/relation matching can be seen as bidirectional. Additionally, edges are weighted, where the weight represents the number of times the pattern extracted the relation.

Formally, we have the bipartite graph $G = (P, R, E)$, with two partitions: P, which contains

[2]We use lemmas instead of the verbatim words for lexical items in the paths, and universal dependencies for the syntactic annotations. Our method accommodates seed relations provided without a predicate, in which case we generate syntactic paths that simply connect the agent and patient.

[3]This database contains psycholinguistic concreteness norms for 40,000 generally known English lemmas on a numerical scale from 1 (highly abstract) to 5 (highly concrete).

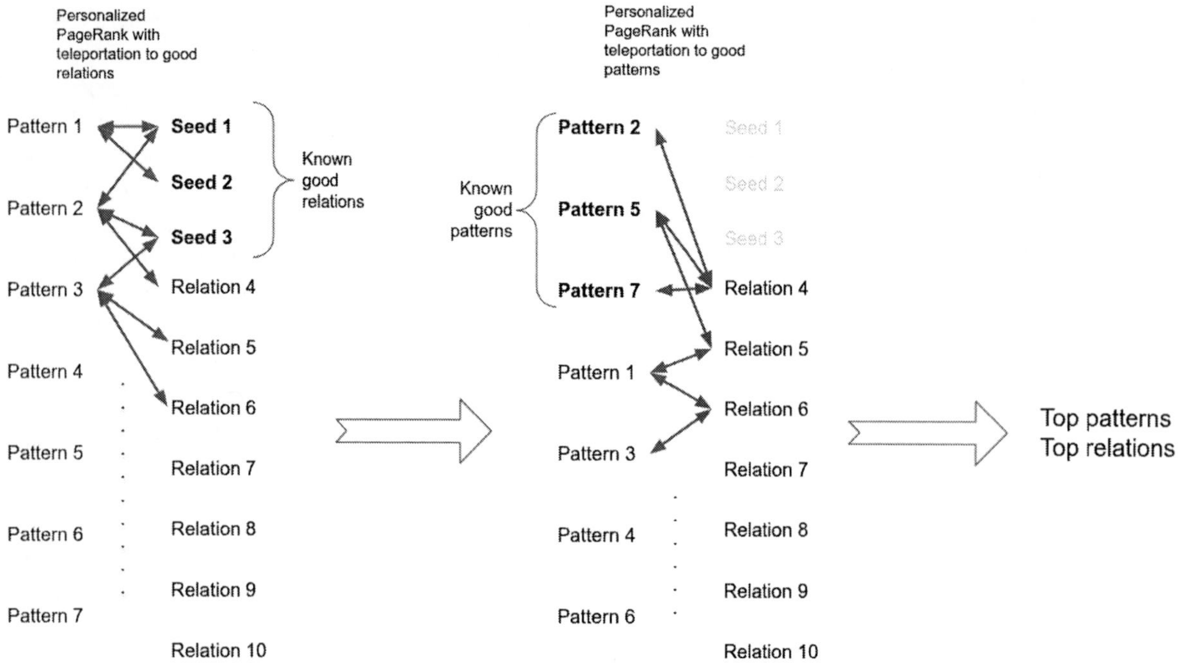

Figure 1: Our proposed method for jointly scoring patterns and relations. We apply the personalized PageRank algorithm twice. First, we use a teleportation vector where we teleport only to the seed relations, i.e., example relations known to be correct. After this step, we take the top scoring patterns and consider them to be correct. We apply the personalized PageRank algorithm a second time, but this time we teleport only to the previously selected patterns. The algorithm outputs a list of patterns and relations, each with an associated score.

the nodes corresponding to the patterns, and R, which has the nodes corresponding to the relations that were extracted using the patterns from P. An undirected edge $(p, r) \in E$ between a pattern $p \in P$ and an extracted relation $r \in R$ is added if the pattern p matches the relation r in the corpora. We attach a weight $w \in \mathbb{N}$ to the (p, r) edge, representing the number of time p extracted r.

Equipped with this representation, we apply graph-based algorithms for jointly scoring the patterns and the relations. We adapt Topic-Sensitive PageRank (Haveliwala, 2002), a variant of PageRank (Page et al., 1999) with custom teleportation probabilities. We apply this algorithm twice, as follows:

1. We first apply it to obtain the scores for each of the generated patterns. In this setting, we set the teleportation probability to uniformly teleport *only* to seed relations, i.e., extractions specified ahead of time by the user to be correct.

2. Using the PageRank scores generated in the previous step, we select the desired number of patterns by keeping the top patterns with the highest scores.

3. We apply the topic-sensitive PageRank a second time. For this run, we teleport *only* to the patterns selected in the previous step. Further, this time we do not teleport uniformly, but proportional with the score of a given pattern. This is done to prevent a pattern which extracted very few relations to dominate the random walk.

At the end of this process, the algorithm generates scores for both patterns and relations. Figure 1 summarizes this whole process.

An important thing to note is that our proposed method considers the entire topology for computing a score, without ignoring or considering an unknown extraction to be bad. As a consequence, a pattern which rarely matches the seed relations can still obtain a high score if its matches tend to overlap with patterns that predominantly match the seed relations. Traditional bootstrapping approaches for relation extraction typically mark unknown extractions as bad, ignore them, or (better) try to score them relative to the seed relations (Gupta and Manning, 2014). In a sense, we handle this problem via a guided wisdom of the crowd approach, where patterns which overlap in extractions with patterns that match predominantly the seed relations can

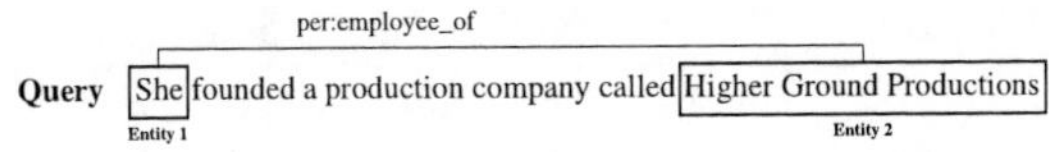

Figure 2: Example of a sentence in the TACRED dataset (Zhang et al., 2017). The task is to predict the relation that holds between the two entities, which in this example is `per:employee_of`.

still obtain a high score.

5 Experiments

5.1 Experimental Setting

For all experiments we used Odinson for indexing (Valenzuela-Escárcega et al., 2020). Further, we used the UMBC corpus (Han et al., 2013) to obtain more robust statistics on a rule's extractions.

5.2 Relation Extraction

We evaluate PatternRank, our proposed method, on the Few-Shot TACRED dataset (Sabo et al., 2021), a few-shot variant of the original TACRED dataset (Zhang et al., 2017). TACRED is a relation classification task, where you are asked to predict the relation between the two (given) entities in a sentence.[4] An example of the input is presented in Figure 2. In the few-shot variant, the test relation classes are *not seen* during training. Instead, a method has to generalize to new relation types using only a few examples of the new relations.[5] More formally, at testing time, the task requires the classification of a relation that holds between two given entities in a *query sentence*, using only a *support set*, which consists of examples for each of the 5 possible relations for the query sentence. If none of the relations hold for the query sentence, the prediction should be `no_relation`.

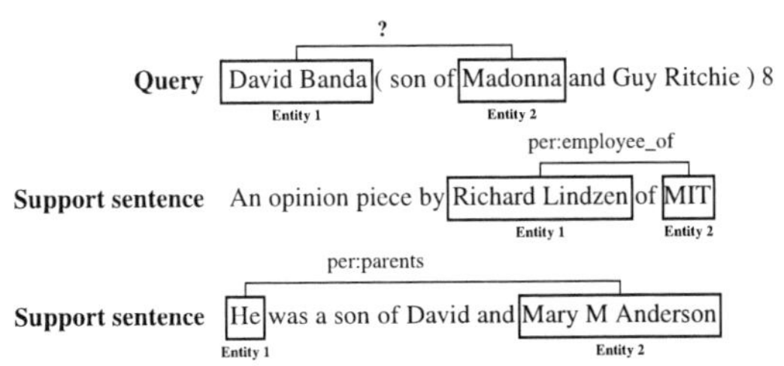

Figure 3: A shortened test example of Few-Shot TACRED. Here, we consider only two support sentences in total, which makes it a 2-way 1-shot setting. If the true relation of the query sentence is not found among the support sentences, then the label is `no_relation`. In this example the gold relation is `per:parents`.

[4]Entity types are also provided.

[5]Typically 1 or 5 sentences per relation.

Because our method starts from seed patterns or relations, we convert each support sentence into seed patterns[6] by artificially constructing patterns that extract the specified entities. We construct two such patterns, one which contains only surface constraints, and one that relies on syntax. For example, for the relation type *per:city_of_birth* and the support sentence ***Rothman** was born in **San Francisco** in 1932*, we automatically generate the surface pattern: `[ne=PER] [lemma=be] [lemma=born] [lemma=in] [ne=LOC]`, and the syntactic pattern: `[ne=PER] <nsubjpass [lemma=born] >nmod_in [ne=LOC]`. We then use UMBC (Han et al., 2013) to obtain robust statistics on their extractions, by making use of the seeds and the relations available so far. More precisely, we apply the patterns on UMBC and extract candidate relations. Then, we use this set of candidate relations to build more patterns. Lastly, we apply this set of patterns over UMBC to obtain the extractions which will then ranked.

We compare our proposed approach with one strong baseline, and several state-of-the-art neural methods.

Our baseline is driven by the type of the two participating entities. In particular, given a query sentence q, which has the entity types $(E1, E2)$ (e.g. (PER, PER) for the example in Figure 3), the algorithm:

1. Discards the sentences from the support set which do not have the entity types $(E1, E2)$. For example, for the example in Figure 3, we discard the first support sentence, as the entity types in it are (PER, ORG).

2. Adds one artificial support sentence with the relation type set to `no_relation`, if in the background training set there are sentences with the same entity types as the query sentence. We do this to ensure that the `no_relation` label remains a classification option, as there may be multiple relations that can hold between the two entities.[7] For example, we add *His son **Richmond Jr** and grandson **Richmond III** both became football stars.* with the relation label `no_relation`.

[6]We empirically observed that seed patterns are less noisy than seed relations.

[7]Examples of relations that can hold between PER and PER: `per:parents`, `per:spouse`, `per:children`, `per:siblings`, `per:other_family`.

3. Randomly picks one of the remaining sentences with matching entity types from the support set, and labels the query sentence with the corresponding relation type. For example, the baseline may randomly select the sentence ***He** was a son of David and **Mary M Anderson***, and predict `per:parents`.

Additionally, we compare our method with the following state-of-the-art supervised methods:

Sentence-Pair (Gao et al., 2019): Concatenates the query sentence with each support sentence and runs a sequence classification variant of BERT (Devlin et al., 2018) over it, predicting a two-element vector. The first element represents the probability of the pair sharing the same relation type and the second element represents the probability of the pair not sharing the same relation type. It takes the average score in case there are multiple sentences with the same relation type. Additionally, the score for `no_relation` is considered to be the smallest value assigned by the method for the probability that the pair does not share the same relation type.

Threshold (Sabo et al., 2021): Assigns the label `no_relation` if the score of the concatenation is smaller than a learned threshold. Otherwise, it assigns the relation type associated with the highest similarity score, as in Sentence-Pair.

NAV (Sabo et al., 2021): A transformer-based classifier which uses the background training set to learn a vector for the `no_relation` label. At test time, it computes the similarity score between the query sentence and each support sentence. Additionally, it computes the similarity score between the query sentence and the vector associated with `no_relation`. Finally, it outputs the relation associated with the highest score.

MNAV (Sabo et al., 2021): Conceptually similar with *NAV*, but instead of using a single vector for the `no_relation` label, it uses multiple vectors. The rationale behind adding multiple vectors is that it is expected to ease the embedding space constraints. The number of vectors is treated as a hyperparameter.

We present our results in Table 1. Note that our method obtains 12.72 F1 in the more challenging 5-way 1-shot setting (where only 1 support sentence is provided per relation label), and 22.13 F1 in the 5-way 5-shot setting (where 5 sentences are provided per type) using 100 patterns. The fact that our method outperforms all others in the 1-shot setting, indicates that our graph-based algorithm generalizes better in the minimal supervision setting. We discuss the results in detail below.

Method	5-way 1-shot	5-way 5-shot
Baseline	10.82±0.01%	10.90±0.01%
Riloff (5)	4.55±0.61%	15.28± 1.71
Riloff (100)	11.68±0.80%	22.01± 1.76
Sentence-Pair	10.19±0.81%	–
Threshold	6.87±0.48%	13.57±0.46%
NAV	8.38±0.80%	18.38±2.01%
MNAV	12.39±1.01%	**30.04**±**1.92%**
Ours (5)	6.53±0.49%	17.05± 1.87 %
Ours (100)	12.72±1.12%	22.13± 1.94 %
Ours (all rules)	**14.06**±0.96%	22.16± 1.67 %

Table 1: Performance comparison between our proposed method, a baseline driven by entity types, Riloff's RlogF approach (Riloff, 1996), and other state-of-the-art neural methods. For both Riloff and our method, we report the results using 5 and 100 patterns learned by the two approaches. Additionally, we add the performance when using all patterns.

6 Analysis and Discussion

6.1 PatternRank vs. Neural Methods

The results in Table 1 show that our method outperforms (or, at least, performs equivalently with) all neural methods in the 1-shot setting, and performs competitively in the 5-shot one. Using all rules we obtain a performance of 14.06 in the harder 5-way 1-shot case, outperforming the previous state-of-the-art of 12.39 by over 1.5 F1 points. This strong performance is preserved even if we use only 100 rules.[8] This confirms our intuition that there is value in graph-based approaches in the neural era, especially in settings with minimal supervision, which are closer to real-world applications of relation extraction. Our conjecture is that teleportation reduces sparsity by allowing patterns that overlap with patterns that predominantly match the seed relations to obtain a high score. At a high level, this approach acts akin to a guided wisdom of the crowd.

Importantly, note that our method produces a relatively small number of interpretable rules, which is a radical departure from these neural methods. We argue that this is a step forward towards reducing the high maintainability cost of neural systems.

One potential argument against our method is that it needs an external text corpus at training time. For example, in this work we used UMBC (Han

[8]Using the top 100 rules per support sentence translates to using approximately 13% of all the patterns found.

et al., 2013). However, so do neural methods: all neural methods reported here rely on transformer networks, which have been pretrained on much larger resources than the corpus we used.

6.2 PatternRank vs. Riloff's RlogF

We compare the scores proposed by our method with the scores proposed by the RlogF scoring function Riloff (1996), which is closest in spirit to our direction. We do not include in this analysis other bootstrapping approaches, such as (Gupta and Manning, 2014; Collins and Singer, 1999), which focus on other NLP tasks, such as named entity recognition. RlogF takes into consideration the number of times a rule matched a seed compared to the total number of matches, as follows:

$$RlogF(pattern_i) = \frac{F_i}{N_i} \cdot log_2(F_i)$$

where F_i is the number of times $pattern_i$ matched a known good relation and N_i is the total number of matches of $pattern_i$. This scoring function treats each pattern in isolation and considers every match outside the seed set as negative.

As Table 1 shows, our approach outperforms RlogF when using 5 patterns and 100 patterns respectively.[9] When using only 5 rules, our proposed approach gives a 40% relative improvement. When using 100 rules, our proposed approach improves RlogF by over 1 F1 points. Overall, we perform much better with few rules and when data is sparse, but our proposed approach outperforms Rlogf in all our experiments, regardless of the setting.

To better understand the differences between the two approaches, we perform an analysis on the patterns resulted from the support sentences of Few-Shot TACRED dev partition. That is, for each support sentence we learn patterns that will be representative for that particular relation. Each pattern has an associated score, given by our proposed method. In the process, we keep track of the number of good and total matches respectively, which are used in RlogF. When comparing the performance, we repeat our experiments 5 times and report the mean and standard deviation. We used the 5-way 1-shot split, unless otherwise stated.

6.2.1 Score agreement

First, we compare the agreement between the scores assigned by both methods. Since we are interested in ranking and not in the values of the scores, we use the Kendall rank correlation coefficient. Naively calculating Kendall's tau between the scores given by RlogF and the scores given by PatternRank yields $\tau = 0.98 \pm 0.02$. However, this is misleading because both scoring methods tend to agree for the low-scoring patterns, which represents the majority of the cases. If, instead, we restrict our analysis to patterns that match seed relations, we obtain $\tau = -0.19 \pm 0.07$.[10] This indicates that the rankings are more dissimilar than the naive ranking would suggest. Manually inspecting the scoring, we observed that RlogF favors high precision patterns, regardless of the number of matches. For example, for the relation *org:country_of_headquarters*, our method scored `[ne=ORG] [lemma=in] [ne=LOC]` the highest, while RlogF scored `[ne=ORG] <conj_and [lemma=president] >nmod_of [ne=LOC]` the highest.

In order to better understand why RlogF over emphasizes precision, we mathematically compared what it means for $pattern_j$ to be scored higher than $pattern_i$ according to this algorithm. Assuming that the $pattern_i$ is known, starting from $RlogF(pattern_i) - RLogF(pattern_j) < 0$, assuming $F_i, F_j, N_i, N_j > 0$ and defining: $\alpha = \frac{F_i}{N_i}$, where $0 < \alpha \leq 1$, and $\beta = \frac{F_j}{N_j}$, where $0 < \beta \leq 1$, we have: $\alpha log_2(F_i) < \beta log_2(F_j)$, and, thus, $F_i < F_j^{\frac{\beta}{\alpha}}$. As such, if α is close to 1 (i.e., the expected value for correct patterns), $pattern_j$ needs exponentially more correct matches the smaller β gets. For example, if $F_i = 100, \alpha = 1$, for a $\beta = 0.75$ we would need $F_j = 465$.

We show the histogram of the resulting scores from both methods in Figure 4. Because RLogF is an unbounded score, we normalize the rule scores between $[0, 1]$. Additionally, we consider only the sentences which resulted in more than 20 patterns, in order to have robust statistics across sentences.[11] We observe that our proposed method produces scores that are more spread in the domain.

Additionally, we note that RlogF scored a higher number of patterns in the higher end of the spectrum ($[0.8, 1]$) than our proposed method. Manu-

[9]We omit running RlogF with all the rules because there is limited benefit of ranking if everything is used, regardless of score. As such, when using all the rules both methods obtain the same score, as they should.

[10]Additionally, RlogF gives a score of 0 for patterns that did not match at least 2 times any seed relations.

[11]That includes over 80% of the sentences.

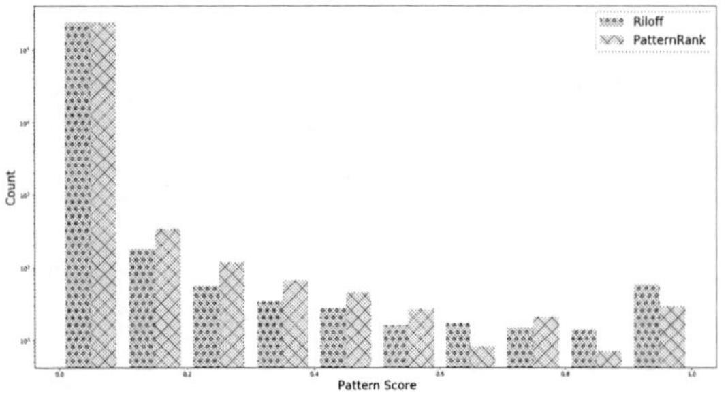

Figure 4: Histogram of scores for the obtained patterns, scored with RlogF and PatternRank. For robust statistics, we consider only sentences which result in more than 20 patterns. Additionally, we normalize the pattern scores per sentence to be in $[0, 1]$. We show the count in log scale for increased visibility.

ally analyzing such cases, we observe that RlogF tends to assign a high scores to patterns with low number of total matches N_i, if its precision F_i is high. When the good matches are sparse in the corpora, this can result in rules that matched only a few times the relations of interest to obtain a high score, when compared with the other rules.[12] This is in line with our previous observation that RLogF over-emphasizes precision.

6.2.2 Pattern importance

Following the observation in Section 6.2.1 that RlogF tends to score more patterns higher than our proposed method, we investigated the performance of the system when taking the n highest-scoring patterns, with both our method and RlogF. We show the results in Figure 5. We note that our method outperforms RlogF consistently until the number of patterns for each sentence gets saturated. We interpret this as further evidence that RlogF assigns overly optimistic scores to patterns with high precision, which can be detrimental when the statistics are not robust.

6.2.3 Random Jump Probability

Our proposed method makes use of the random jump probability, which ensures that the resulting matrix is ergodic. We assess the influence of this hyper-parameter by analyzing the performance of the method when varying it. We set the number of patterns used for each method to 10. As highlighted in Figure 6, we found our system to be robust to hyper-parameter changes, outperforming RlogF for

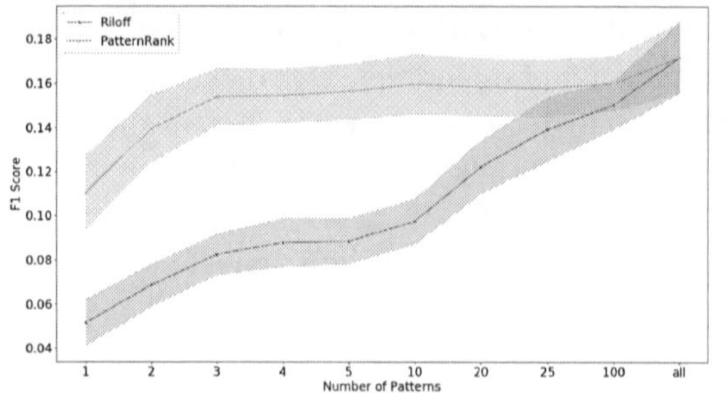

Figure 5: Performance of our method compared with RlogF, varying the number of patterns accepted. We note that our proposed method consistently outperforms RLogF up until the number of patterns are saturated.

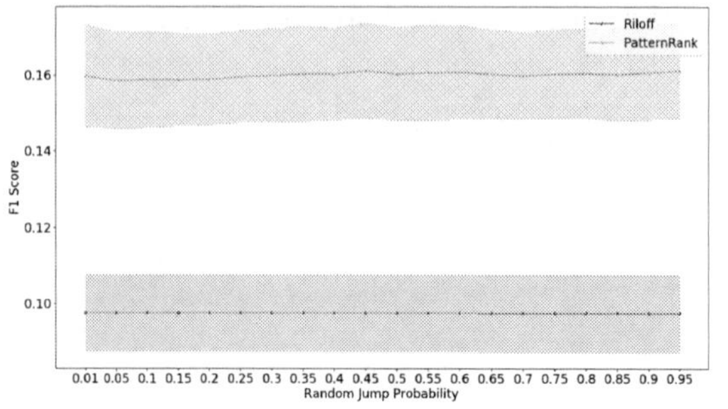

Figure 6: Performance of our method compared with RlogF, when varying the random jump probability. We used the top 10 best patterns according to each method. We average over all the dev episodes. We note that our proposed method consistently outperforms RLogF, and that the performance is robust to changes in the random jump probability.

all the values we tested.[13]

6.3 Resulting Rules

Quantitatively, our proposed method outperforms Riloff on the relation classification task regardless of the number of patterns considered. Qualitatively, analyzing the top scored patterns, we observe that our proposed method tends to prefer patterns which offer a better balance between precision and recall due to using the whole topology of the pattern/relation graph. We show a few examples of the top scored patterns with both methods in Table 2 for two relations from development: `org:country_of_headquarters` and `per:age`.

6.4 Limitations

Our proposed method provides some advantages, such as simplicity and greater interpretability. Nevertheless, it has some limitations. First, our pro-

[12]Changing $\frac{F_i}{N_i} \cdot log_2(F_i)$ to $\frac{F_i}{N_i} \cdot log_2(N_i)$ does not change the histogram, nor the performance.

[13]A random jump probability of 0 is not possible because then the graph might not be connected. A random jump probability of 1 is not useful because it translates to jumping from node to node, randomly.

Relations: org:country_of_headquarters
PatternRank (ours):
[ne=ORG]+ [lemma=in] [ne=LOC]+
[ne=ORG]+ [lemma=","] [ne=LOC]+
Riloff:
[ne=ORG]+ <nmod:poss [lemma=campaign] >nmod_against [ne=LOC]+
[ne=ORG]+ <appos [lemma=institute] >nmod_in [ne=LOC]+

Relations: per:age
PatternRank (ours):
[ne=PER]+ [lemma=","] [ne=NUMBER]+
[ne=PER]+ [lemma=be] [ne=NUMBER]+
Riloff:
[ne=PER]+ >appos [lemma=kan] >nummod [ne=NUMBER]+
[ne=PER]+ >appos [lemma=student] >det:qmod [ne=NUMBER]+

Table 2: Comparison between the top scoring patterns according to our method and to RlogF. We observe that our proposed method tends to score higher patterns that generalize better, i.e., patterns with fewer lexical or syntactic constraints.

posed method depends on an external explicit corpus. Typical pre-trained LMs compress the underlying text used for training in its parameters, while our proposed method needs the explicit text.

Second, our assumption that the same relation holds between entities of type (ENTITY1,ENTITY2) might not always be true. Nevertheless, this assumption was empirically proven using distant supervision (Mintz et al., 2009). Our empirical results add evidence to its efficacy. However, this assumption must be evaluated before employing this method in downstream applications.

Third, though rules are generally less prone to overfitting and offer good out-of-domain generalization, they may have limited expressivity when compared to neural methods. Nevertheless, the capacity needs of a model should be evaluated on a per-application basis. For example, (Tang and Surdeanu, 2023) found that using only rules can achieve a performance of over 65% F1 on the supervised TACRED task. This is comparable to state-of-the-art neural methods, which by now obtain 70+% F1,[14] suggesting that rule-based methods can be competitive on information extraction tasks.

[14]https://paperswithcode.com/sota/relation-extraction-on-tacred

7 Conclusion

We propose a new pattern acquisition method for relation extraction, which uses graph-based techniques that operate over the entire topology of the bipartite graph that contains candidate patterns and their extracted relations.

We evaluate our proposed approach on the Few-Shot TACRED task (Sabo et al., 2021), a more realistic and harder variant of TACRED (Zhang et al., 2017). Our proposed approach outperforms or performs comparably with more opaque neural methods. Further, we empirically show that our proposed method performs better than the seminal pattern scoring method proposed in (Riloff, 1996), RLogF. Lastly, we highlight some of the limitations of our proposed approach.

All in all, we provide compelling evidence that, for specific applications, rule-based methods continue to offer comparable or better performance than their neural counterparts, and, thus, they should not be overlooked by current and future research on information extraction.

Acknowledgments

This work was partially supported by the National Science Foundation (NSF) under grant #2006583. Mihai Surdeanu declares a financial interest in lum.ai. This interest has been properly disclosed to the University of Arizona Institutional Review Committee and is managed in accordance with its conflict of interest policies.

References

Anders Arpteg, Björn Brinne, Luka Crnkovic-Friis, and J. Bosch. 2018. Software engineering challenges of deep learning. *2018 44th Euromicro Conference on Software Engineering and Advanced Applications (SEAA)*, pages 50–59.

Sergey Brin. 1998. Extracting patterns and relations from the world wide web. In *WebDB*.

Marc Brysbaert, Amy Beth Warriner, and Victor Kuperman. 2014. Concreteness ratings for 40 thousand generally known english word lemmas. *Behavior research methods*, 46(3):904–911.

Michael Collins and Yoram Singer. 1999. Unsupervised models for named entity classification. In *EMNLP*.

Jacob Devlin, Ming-Wei Chang, Kenton Lee, and Kristina Toutanova. 2018. BERT: pre-training of deep bidirectional transformers for language understanding. *CoRR*, abs/1810.04805.

Tianyu Gao, Xu Han, Hao Zhu, Zhiyuan Liu, Peng Li, Maosong Sun, and Jie Zhou. 2019. Fewrel 2.0: Towards more challenging few-shot relation classification. In *EMNLP/IJCNLP*.

S. Gupta and Christopher D. Manning. 2014. Improved pattern learning for bootstrapped entity extraction. In *CoNLL*.

Lushan Han, Abhay Lokesh Kashyap, Timothy W. Finin, James Mayfield, and Jonathan Weese. 2013. Umbc_ebiquity-core: Semantic textual similarity systems. In **SEMEVAL*.

Hany Hassan, Ahmed Hassan Awadallah, and Ossama Emam. 2006. Unsupervised information extraction approach using graph mutual reinforcement. In *EMNLP*.

Taher H. Haveliwala. 2002. Topic-sensitive pagerank. In *Proceedings of the 11th International Conference on World Wide Web*, WWW '02, page 517–526, New York, NY, USA. Association for Computing Machinery.

Marti A. Hearst. 1992. Automatic acquisition of hyponyms from large text corpora. In *COLING 1992 Volume 2: The 14th International Conference on Computational Linguistics*.

Sarthak Jain and Byron C. Wallace. 2019. Attention is not explanation. *CoRR*, abs/1902.10186.

Jon M. Kleinberg. 1999. Hubs, authorities, and communities. *ACM Comput. Surv.*, 31:5.

Goro Kobayashi, Tatsuki Kuribayashi, Sho Yokoi, and Kentaro Inui. 2020. Attention module is not only a weight: Analyzing transformers with vector norms. *CoRR*, abs/2004.10102.

Zornitsa Kozareva, Ellen Riloff, and Eduard H. Hovy. 2008. Semantic class learning from the web with hyponym pattern linkage graphs. In *ACL*.

Dekang Lin and Patrick Pantel. 2001. Dirt @sbt@discovery of inference rules from text. In *Proceedings of the Seventh ACM SIGKDD International Conference on Knowledge Discovery and Data Mining*, KDD '01, page 323–328, New York, NY, USA. Association for Computing Machinery.

Christopher D. Manning. 2015. Computational linguistics and deep learning. *Computational Linguistics*, 41:701–707.

R. Thomas McCoy, Ellie Pavlick, and Tal Linzen. 2019. Right for the wrong reasons: Diagnosing syntactic heuristics in natural language inference. *CoRR*, abs/1902.01007.

Mike D. Mintz, Steven Bills, Rion Snow, and Dan Jurafsky. 2009. Distant supervision for relation extraction without labeled data. In *ACL*.

Lawrence Page, Sergey Brin, Rajeev Motwani, and Terry Winograd. 1999. The pagerank citation ranking: Bringing order to the web. Technical Report 1999-66, Stanford InfoLab. Previous number = SIDL-WP-1999-0120.

Ellen Riloff. 1993. Automatically constructing a dictionary for information extraction tasks. In *AAAI*.

Ellen Riloff. 1996. Automatically generating extraction patterns from untagged text. In *AAAI/IAAI, Vol. 2*.

Ellen Riloff and R. Jones. 1999. Learning dictionaries for information extraction by multi-level bootstrapping. In *AAAI/IAAI*.

Ellen Riloff and Janyce Wiebe. 2003. Learning extraction patterns for subjective expressions. In *EMNLP*.

O. Mahamane Sani Sabo, Yanai Elazar, Yoav Goldberg, and Ido Dagan. 2021. Revisiting few-shot relation classification: Evaluation data and classification schemes. *Transactions of the Association for Computational Linguistics*, 9:691–706.

D. Sculley, Gary Holt, Daniel Golovin, Eugene Davydov, Todd Phillips, Dietmar Ebner, Vinay Chaudhary, Michael Young, Jean-François Crespo, and Dan Dennison. 2015. Hidden technical debt in machine learning systems. In *NIPS*.

Zheng Tang and Mihai Surdeanu. 2023. It takes two flints to make a fire: Multitask learning of neural relation and explanation classifiers. *Computational Linguistics*. Accepted on 2022.

Marco A. Valenzuela-Escárcega, Gus Hahn-Powell, and Dane Bell. 2020. Odinson: A fast rule-based information extraction framework. In *Proceedings of the 12th Language Resources and Evaluation Conference*, pages 2183–2191, Marseille, France. European Language Resources Association.

Sarah Wiegreffe and Yuval Pinter. 2019. Attention is not not explanation. *CoRR*, abs/1908.04626.

Yuhao Zhang, Victor Zhong, Danqi Chen, Gabor Angeli, and Christopher D. Manning. 2017. Position-aware attention and supervised data improve slot filling. In *Proceedings of the 2017 Conference on Empirical Methods in Natural Language Processing (EMNLP 2017)*, pages 35–45.

Key Information Extraction in Purchase Documents using Deep Learning and Rule-based Corrections

Roberto Arroyo, Javier Yebes, Elena Martínez, Héctor Corrales, Javier Lorenzo
NielsenIQ Spain
{roberto.arroyo,javier.yebes,elena.martinez,hector.corrales,javier.lorenzo}@nielseniq.com

Abstract

Deep Learning (DL) is dominating the fields of Natural Language Processing (NLP) and Computer Vision (CV) in the recent times. However, DL commonly relies on the availability of large data annotations, so other alternative or complementary pattern-based techniques can help to improve results. In this paper, we build upon Key Information Extraction (KIE) in purchase documents using both DL and rule-based corrections. Our system initially trusts on Optical Character Recognition (OCR) and text understanding based on entity tagging to identify purchase facts of interest (e.g., product codes, descriptions, quantities, or prices). These facts are then linked to a same product group, which is recognized by means of line detection and some grouping heuristics. Once these DL approaches are processed, we contribute several mechanisms consisting of rule-based corrections for improving the baseline DL predictions. We prove the enhancements provided by these rule-based corrections over the baseline DL results in the presented experiments for purchase documents from public and NielsenIQ datasets.

1 Introduction

The intersection between NLP and CV algorithms is a key factor in systems that require processing visual and textual features. There are several use cases in the retailing industry in which this combination is typically applied, such as automated item coding (Arroyo et al., 2019), classification of promotions in digital leaflets (Arroyo et al., 2020) or the application of Visual Question Answering (VQA) to store observation systems (Arroyo et al., 2022), among others. In general terms, a great part of these use cases rely on KIE for automatically obtaining data of interest from varied sources related to images and documents. One of the main approaches based on KIE for retail and consumer measurement is focused on the automated recognition of data from purchase documents, such as receipts and invoices.

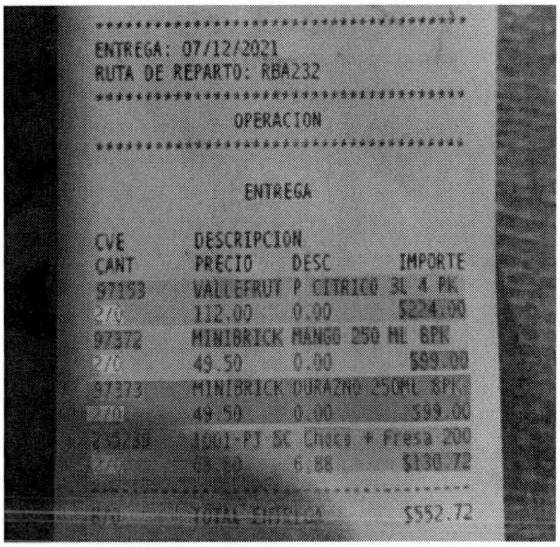

Figure 1: Example of KIE in purchase documents from the NielsenIQ dataset. We can see entities tagged as product codes in gray, descriptions in green, quantities in yellow and total prices in red. Moreover, the regions corresponding to a same product jointly with their linked entities are marked in a blue to purple scale.

The information of interest commonly acquired by purchase decoding systems is associated with the purchased products printed in the documents to be recognized at item level, as depicted in Fig. 1. Here, there are several entities of text related to the characteristics of a purchased product that are generally extracted, such as the following ones:

- *Description*: textual specification for representing a purchased product.
- *Code*: unique numerical identifier of a purchased product.
- *Quantity*: total purchased units of the same product.
- *Price*: total value of all the purchased units from the same product.

Proceedings of the 29th International Conference on Computational Linguistic, pages 11–20
October 12–17, 2022.

In this paper, we propose a novel approach for KIE in purchase documents using DL and rule-based corrections. The presented DL architecture initially extracts the words contained in the document using OCR facilities. The recognized words jointly with the processed image are used as input of an entity tagging model based on Transformers and Convolutional Neural Networks (CNNs), which is able to predict the facts associated with the purchased products. Then, we compute a line detection method based on GNNs (Graph Neural Networks) with the aim of grouping all the text lines corresponding to a same product for entity linking. Finally, our pipeline applies some rule-based refinements to the previously predicted tags to correct possible inconsistencies.

We observed that standard DL proposals for entity tagging decrease their performance in complex purchase documents with low image quality, so false positives and false negatives commonly appear within the set of predictions. However, we know some specific business rules related to purchase documents for product descriptions, codes, quantities and prices that can be applied in post-processing, with the aim of enhancing the global accuracy of the system. In this way, we can take advantage of the patterns learned by DL and combine them with the human knowledge about the rules related to the purchase document decoding use case, so both can be applied in a complementary way to improve the quality of our whole solution.

In this regard, the main contributions derived from the research presented in this paper are the following ones:

- Design of a DL approach for KIE focused on purchase documents, which fuses NLP and CV in an architecture composed of OCR, entity tagging and product line grouping for entity linking.
- Definition of rule-based corrections in order to enhance the initial predictions given by the DL approach, demonstrating how pattern-based techniques can complement DL to improve performance.
- Presentation of a set of experiments in public and NielsenIQ datasets with the aim of validating our DL approach for KIE in purchase documents, jointly with the enhancements provided by rule-based corrections.

The contents of the paper are organized as follows: a review of the main state-of-the-art methods for KIE in document decoding is presented in Section 2. Our approach for KIE in purchase documents using DL and rule-based corrections is detailed in Section 3. The main experiments and results related to our DL proposal and the accuracy improvements of rule-based corrections are discussed in Section 4. The final conclusions associated with our research and some insights about future works are finally summarized in Section 5.

2 Related Work

The rise of DL has provided powerful tools to the fields of NLP and CV, which are the base of KIE systems focused on purchase documents decoding. This research line has also grown thanks to the proliferation of related public datasets, such as CORD (Park et al., 2019), SROIE (Huang et al., 2019) or FUNSD (Jaume et al., 2019). Moreover, companies working on retail intelligence also generate large amounts of data that are typically used for researching in real use cases, such as NielsenIQ.

In the intersection between NLP and CV, OCR techniques commonly represent the starting point for recognizing the text contained in a document or image. Methods based on OCR examine images pixel by pixel, looking for shapes that match the character traits. The state of the art in OCR comprises solutions that are open source and proprietary. Tesseract OCR is one of the most effective open-source approaches (Anwar et al., 2022). However, proprietary solutions such as Amazon or Google OCR are currently obtaining much better results in text recognition (Hegghammer, 2022).

Once the text is recognized, purchase document decoding systems typically need to understand certain parts or extract specific information. In this regard, the recent popularization of Transformers (Vaswani et al., 2017) and architectures such as BERT (Devlin et al., 2018) in the NLP community has provided new tools for achieving the desired results.

Among the different possibilities of text understanding, document decoding systems for purchase facts are commonly associated with entity tagging. This approach is applied with the aim of extracting specific product information in purchase documents, such as product description, code, quantity or price. Entity tagging is another state-of-the-art field that has been benefited by Transformers.

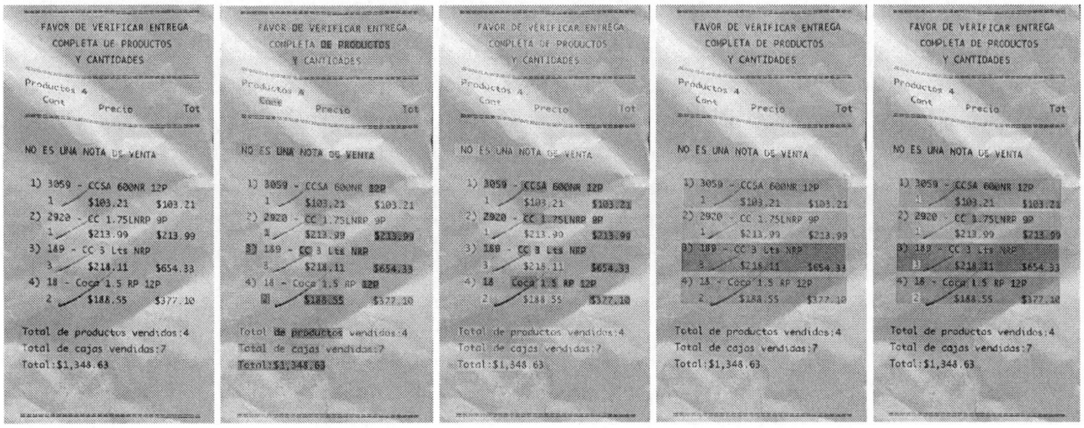

(a) Input. (b) OCR. (c) Entity tagging. (d) Prod. line grouping. (e) Output.

Figure 2: Main stages of our approach for KIE in purchase documents using DL and rule-based corrections. a) Input: initial data acquisition and image digitalization. b) OCR: detection and recognition of the words in the image. c) Entity tagging: identification of purchase facts of interest (e.g., product codes, descriptions, quantities, or prices). d) Product line grouping: identification of text lines and grouping by products of interest. e) Output: final predictions after rule-based corrections (if any). In this case, the diagram shows an example were DL was enough to properly predict all the tags, but we will depict specific cases along the paper in which rule-based corrections are carried out with respect to the original entity tagging predictions.

For instance, the architecture defined by PICK (Yu et al., 2021) is typically used in entity tagging systems, because its combination of Transformers to get text embeddings and CNNs to obtain image embeddings (He et al., 2016) provides one of the top performances in the recent literature. Another popular technique for entity tagging is LayoutLM and its different versions (Xu et al., 2020, 2021a; Huang et al., 2022), including an approach focused on multilingual capabilities (Xu et al., 2021b).

Apart from entity tagging, entity linking is also typically required to match each purchase tag with each respective product in the purchase document. Here, state-of-the-art techniques such as SPADE (Hwang et al., 2021) or BROS (Hong et al., 2022) propose end-to-end entity linking approaches. However, our proposal considers a method based on two stages, consisting of an initial entity tagging which is then linked by using line detection algorithms and rule-based heuristics for product lines grouping. For line detection, we take advantage of recent GNN proposals such as (Qasim et al., 2019) or (Carbonell et al., 2021).

Unfortunately, the state of the art does not consider a lot of solutions for correcting wrong entity tagging predictions, which is something typical in complex documents. For this reason, we propose novel rule-based corrections for improving automated entity tagging in purchase documents.

3 Our Approach

In this section, our whole pipeline proposed for KIE in purchase documents using DL and rule-based corrections is described. The core architecture builds upon DL in order to obtain the initial predictions for recognizing the text in the documents and tag words into varied categories from the different purchased products characteristics. Once these baseline predictions are provided by the DL pipeline, the implemented rule-based corrections are applied to refine the final output. We explain both DL and rule-based schemas with the aim of fully understanding the complementary solutions designed to extract the information of interest from purchase documents.

3.1 DL Architecture

The pipeline based on DL is composed of three main stages presented in Fig. 2 from input to output. These stages are basically OCR, entity tagging and product line grouping.

We explain the most common technical challenges for each stage along this section, jointly with their implementations mainly based on DL approaches. The goal is to understand how the learned textual and visual features are impacting the performance of the final system before checking how rule-based patterns can complement them to enhance the final output.

3.1.1 OCR

The proper selection of a robust OCR engine is crucial for the development of any document decoding system, because it is the bottleneck for the subsequent stages in the DL architecture.

OCR converts purchase images into machine-readable text data. The human visual system reads text by recognizing the patterns of light and dark, translating those patterns into characters and words, and then attaching meaning to it. Similarly, OCR attempts to mimic our visual system by using DL.

As discussed in Section 2, papers focused on benchmarking OCR engines such as (Hegghammer, 2022) have demonstrated that propietary solutions are currently yielding much accurate results than open-source proposals. Then, we decided to build upon the OCR provided by the Google Vision API[1], which provides some of the most remarkable results in text recognition. It must be noted that the goals of this paper are not focused on contributing a new OCR engine, so we decided just to apply Google Vision API features for recognizing text as a base tool for the rest of the stages implemented for KIE in purchase documents using DL.

The output obtained by the OCR service is composed of the recognized text over the images and the locations of the detected characters, words and paragraphs, as shown in the visual example presented in Fig. 3. This output is used as input of the subsequent stage for entity tagging in order to classify the different words into their corresponding categories related to the varied purchased products characteristics.

Figure 3: Visual example of OCR processing using the Google Vision API over a purchase document. Image is focused on a section where purchased products are printed. The output shows the detected characters, words and paragraphs over the image and the recognized text.

[1]https://cloud.google.com/vision

3.1.2 Entity Tagging

KIE systems typically require algorithms to understand the recognized text and categorize some parts of it. In this sense, entity tagging is used with the aim of categorizing information of interest from purchased products, such as descriptions, codes, quantities or prices.

There are different proposals in the recent state of the art for computing entity tagging based on DL. In our pipeline, we follow an encoder-decoder architecture similar to the presented in works such as (Yu et al., 2021). Within this schema, text features are acquired by a Transformer and image features are processed by a CNN, as shown in Fig. 4.

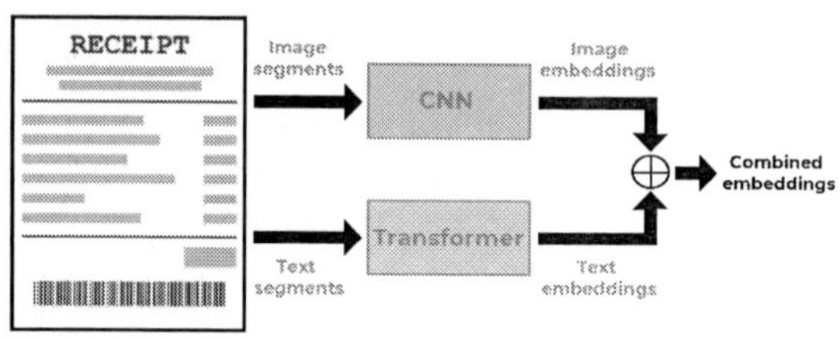

Figure 4: Base architecture for entity tagging using DL. Tranformers and CNNs are applied for extracting text and image embeddings, respectively.

The combined embeddings (CE) are obtained by fusing the image (IE) and text (TE) embeddings using an element-wise addition operation, as formulated in Eq. 1. Previously, IE and TE are outputted by the encoders into a vector derived from the CNN ($ie^{(x)}$) and Transformer ($te^{(x)}$) features respectively, as shown in Eq. 2 and Eq. 3. The encoders (θ) in each case are defined in Eq. 4 and Eq. 5, where $is^{(x)}$ represents the input image segments and $ts^{(x)}$ the corresponding text segments.

$$CE = IE \oplus TE \tag{1}$$

$$IE = [ie^1, ie^2, ..., ie^{N-1}, ie^N] \tag{2}$$

$$TE = [te^1, te^2, ..., te^{N-1}, te^N] \tag{3}$$

$$ie^{(x)} = \text{cnn}(is^{(x)}, \theta_{cnn}) \tag{4}$$

$$te^{(x)} = \text{transformer}(ts^{(x)}, \theta_{transformer}) \tag{5}$$

It must be noted that we decided to use a DL encoder-decoder architecture based on Transformers and CNNs because it is one of the most successful approaches in the state of the art, as we will discuss in the experiments presented in Section 4. However, our subsequent rule-based corrections over DL predictions could be adapted to any other entity tagging technique focused on similar DL schemas.

3.1.3 Product Line Grouping

Once entity tags are initially recognized for a purchase document, they are grouped by product to know their relationships and association with specific purchase characteristics. This entity linking is performed by applying a product line grouping step that uses DL and some grouping heuristics.

Firstly, the lines of the document must be individually detected. To do this, a GNN based on (Qasim et al., 2019) is implemented with the aim of connecting the different words previously extracted as entity tags of interest in a same line. This GNN proposes an architecture based on graph networks that combines the benefits of CNNs for visual feature extraction and graph networks for dealing with the problem structure.

After detecting the individual lines, some heuristics are applied to group the lines corresponding to a same product, as illustrated in Fig. 5. The steps of this grouping process are the following ones:

1. Take the first individual line detected (from top to bottom in Y axis) and check if there are product description entities. If not, continue searching until the grouping algorithm finds the first line with a product description.

2. Once the algorithm finds the line with product description entities, there are two options:
   (a) If the line also contains a product quantity and price (codes are not always available according to business rules), all the information of interest is located in that line and can be individually grouped.
   (b) If the line only contains description tags, go to step 3.

3. Check if the next line contains another description or any other tag, there are two options:
   (a) If there are only description tags, it means that the whole product description covers more than one line. The algorithm will search until it finds a line containing any other entity different from description before closing the group of lines.
   (b) If there are tags such as product quantity or price, the group of lines can be directly closed. Then, the algorithm takes the previously accumulated lines for the current product and combines their bounding boxes to obtain the final product line grouping.

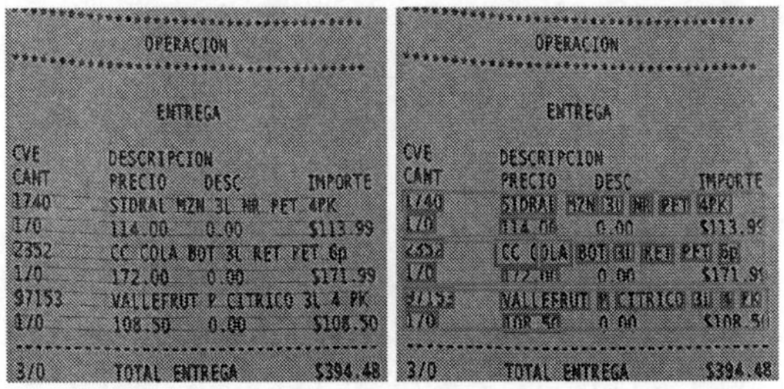

(a) Line detection. (b) Product line grouping.

Figure 5: Visual example from line detection to product line grouping. On the left image, the individual lines detected by the GNN from entities of interest are represented in purple. On the right image, the final product line groups are depicted in red, jointly with the entity tagging words of interest in blue.

3.2 Rule-based Corrections

Current solutions for document decoding trust on DL for varied algorithms related to NLP and CV, as we previously reviewed in our architecture for KIE in purchase documents. Unfortunately, the high variety of formats, qualities and languages in these documents makes difficult to train models able to generalize to every situation. Then, we can expect some errors in the baseline entity tagging predictions provided by a DL pipeline. These errors are not always possible to correct, because in some cases the associated text is very difficult to recognize and understand. However, there are some other cases in which we can apply business rules and human knowledge to find and ameliorate DL errors in predictions.

It is possible to correct some of the missed elements in the initial tags (false negatives) and even the ones that are wrongly detected (false positives) to replace them with the correct ones. Product descriptions are the core of our product line grouping heuristics because they are generally the most accurate in automation and usually contain several words. In the proposed rule-based corrections for entities, we focus on tags that are commonly composed of only one word based on numbers, which are a typical source of issues in purchase document decoding. These entity tags are mainly product codes, product quantities and product prices. It must be noted that although we focus on these common purchase tags, the rule-based corrections presented in this paper could be adapted or updated for other purchase tags depending on the requirements of a specific use case.

3.2.1 Corrections in Product Codes

Product codes do not always appear as part of the product information in purchase documents. However, when they are included among these data, they are typically the highest integer number in a product line grouping, as can be seen in the example presented in Fig. 6. Then, in case we cannot find the product code with the initial DL-based entity tagging, we can re-check if it is available by applying the rule formulated in Eq. 6 and Eq. 7, where TW_{pr} is a vector composed of all the words $(tw_{pr}^{(x)})$ that are not tagged inside a specific product group. It must be noted that $code_{pr}$ will be only corrected if the number resulting from applying Eq. 7 is higher than the minimum integer value among all the remaining words that are not tagged from DL predictions.

$$TW_{pr} = [tw_{pr}^{(1)}, tw_{pr}^{(2)}, ..., tw_{pr}^{(N-1)}, tw_{pr}^{(N)}] \quad (6)$$

$$code_{pr} = \max(\text{integer}(TW_{pr})) \quad (7)$$

In this case, we just try to find the missing code for a product if it has not been previously detected in order to solve false negatives, but it could be also applied for correcting false positives from DL predictions if required. In that scenario, low confidences associated with DL predictions in entity tagging could help to find candidates to be corrected. However, we decided to fix only false negatives and trust on DL for the rest of predictions, with the aim of obtaining the highest benefit from both DL predictions and rule-based corrections, without an implicit dependency on confidence thresholds. In fact, this schema obtains a remarkable enhancement in performance according to the results presented in Section 4.2, without adding the extra complexity and possible issues related to also modifying explicit DL predictions. A similar way of correcting false negatives is proposed for product quantities and prices.

3.2.2 Corrections in Product Quantities

Product quantity is another entity tag typically printed in purchase documents that can be fixed in several cases during post-processing by applying rule-based corrections. In this regard, we must consider that this value usually represents an integer number close or equal to one.

According to the previous considerations, we can search for the lowest integer number in a product line grouping in case we did not initially find this tag with DL-based entity tagging, as depicted in the visual examples that are presented in Fig. 7.

More formally, the definition of the rule associated with this correction for missed product quantities is formulated in Eq. 8. It must be noted that $quantity_{pr}$ will be only corrected if the number resulting from applying Eq. 8 is lower than the maximum integer value among all the remaining words that are not tagged from DL predictions.

$$quantity_{pr} = \min(\text{integer}(TW_{pr})) \quad (8)$$

3.2.3 Corrections in Product Prices

Product prices are commonly represented by float numbers. In the use case exposed along this paper, we specifically tag the total prices per product, so it is expected to find the highest float number in these situations. Then, if DL predictions are not able to find a total price for a product line grouping, the rule-based correction formulated in Eq. 9 is applied to check if it is possible to find a word that is not tagged fulfilling these requirements.

$$price_{pr} = \max(\text{float}(TW_{pr})) \quad (9)$$

4 Experiments

The main goal of the presented experiments is to verify the performance of our DL pipeline for KIE in purchase documents and demonstrate how rule-based corrections can increase final accuracy.

Initially, some public datasets are used to obtain performance metrics with the aim of comparing different entity tagging architectures with respect to our proposal based on an encoder-decoder built upon Transformers and CNNs, which is inspired by (Yu et al., 2021). The goal of this experiment is to validate that even a top state-of-the-art technique for entity tagging based on DL is far from perfection, so rule-based corrections can provide an added value for the most common error cases.

Besides, a dataset acquired by NielsenIQ is used to test the performance of the whole pipeline, including quantitative comparisons related to the improvements provided by rule-based corrections. Some qualitative examples from the NielsenIQ dataset can be reviewed in Figs. 6, 7 and 8.

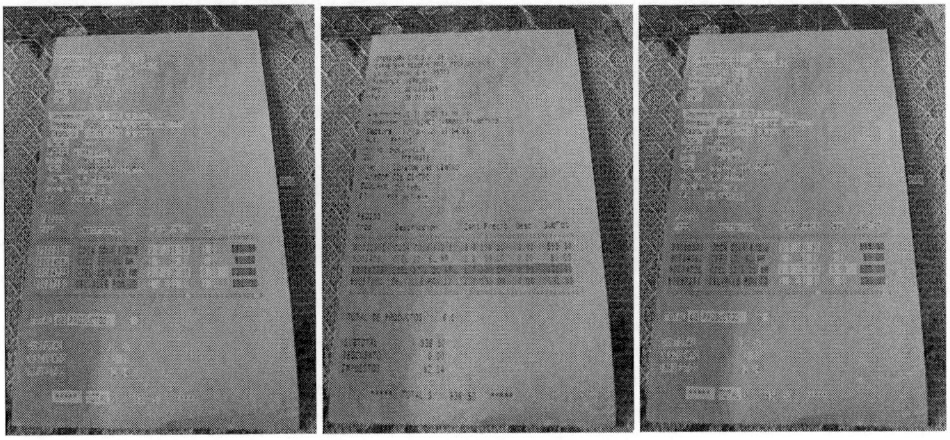

(a) Baseline entities. (b) Product line grouping. (c) Corrected entities for codes.

Figure 6: Visual examples of product code correction (in gray) based on rule-based heuristics.

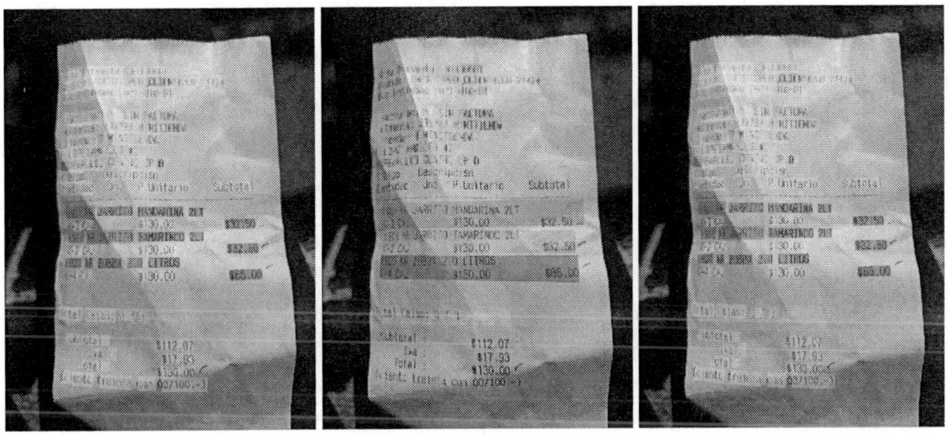

(a) Baseline entities. (b) Product line grouping. (c) Corrected entities for quantities.

Figure 7: Visual examples of product quantity correction (in yellow) based on rule-based heuristics.

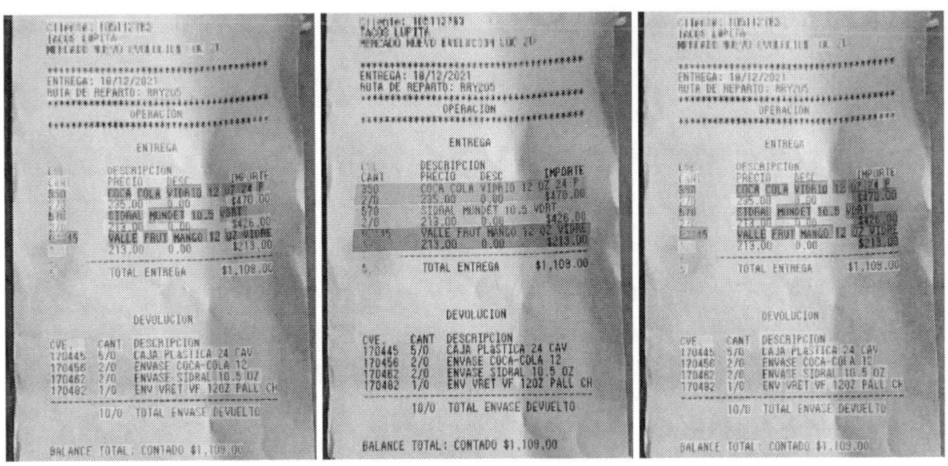

(a) Baseline entities. (b) Product line grouping. (c) Corrected entities for prices.

Figure 8: Visual examples of product price correction (in red) based on rule-based heuristics.

Method	Main reference	Parameters	f1-score		
			CORD	SROIE	FUNSD
BERT	(Devlin et al., 2018)	110M	89.7	91.0	60.7
LayoutLMv1	(Xu et al., 2020)	113M	94.7	94.4	78.6
LayoutLMv2	(Xu et al., 2021a)	200M	94.9	96.2	82.7
LayoutLMv3	(Huang et al., 2022)	133M	96.5	96.4	90.3
LayoutXLM	(Xu et al., 2021b)	345M	95.7	96.1	82.7
SPADE	(Hwang et al., 2021)	110M	91.5	93.2	71.6
BROS	(Hong et al., 2022)	139M	95.3	95.5	81.2
PICK	(Yu et al., 2021)	68M	95.2	96.1	82.5

Table 1: Comparison of state-of-the-art methods for entity tagging in the CORD, SROIE and FUNSD datasets.

4.1 Datasets

The main characteristics of the datasets used in our experiments are briefly reviewed here. The public datasets evaluated are CORD, SROIE and FUNSD. Apart from this, we also perform specific tests for our use case related to KIE in purchase documents by means of the NielsenIQ dataset.

4.1.1 The CORD Dataset

The COnsolidated Receipt Dataset (CORD)[2] is focused on receipt understanding for entity tagging and linking. The dataset includes 800 receipts for the training set, 100 for the validation set and 100 for the test set. A photo and a list of OCR annotations are included for each receipt. For entity tagging, there are 30 classes related to different information from shops and restaurants in Indonesia.

4.1.2 The SROIE Dataset

The Scanned Receipts OCR and Information Extraction (SROIE)[3] dataset is composed of a scanned collection from 1000 store receipts. 600 images are used for training and 400 for testing. Each receipt contains around about four key text fields for entity tagging. The text annotated in the dataset mainly consists of digits and English characters.

4.1.3 The FUNSD Dataset

The Form Understanding in Noisy Scanned Documents (FUNSD)[4] dataset includes documents containing forms. It is composed of 199 scanned documents, where 9707 semantic entities are annotated from 31485 words. 149 images are used for training and 50 for testing. There are 4 semantic entities: header, question, answer and other.

[2] http://github.com/clovaai/cord

[3] http://rrc.cvc.uab.es/?ch=13

[4] http://guillaumejaume.github.io/FUNSD

4.1.4 The NielsenIQ Dataset

Commonly, public datasets related to purchase document decoding include varied tags that are not always fitting the requirements of a particular use case. In our system, we want to specifically decode descriptions, codes, quantities and total prices per product. Then, we have used our own labeled data from NielsenIQ[5] considering the previously specified purchase tags to train and evaluate our full pipeline. As this dataset is composed of proprietary images, we can not publicly share them, but you can check their main characteristics in the example presented in Fig. 1. The images were captured with smartphones in different countries, with more than 10000 samples. Several challenges are considered due to the characteristics of data acquisition, such as different formats per retailer and country, multiple languages, or capturing quality for acquired images (e.g., varied resolutions, shadowing effects, blurring, oclussions, etc.).

4.2 Results

Based on the previously described datasets, we have processed several results regarding the state of the art in entity tagging and our whole KIE pipeline. The final goal is to measure the improvements in our DL system provided by the proposed rule-based corrections.

4.2.1 Entity Tagging Results

In Table 1, the base architectures of several approaches for entity tagging introduced in Section 2 are compared. We analyze the number of parameters for each approach and f1-scores in the public datasets introduced for document decoding (CORD, SROIE and FUNSD).

[5] http://nielseniq.com

Experiments for entity tagging	f1-score				
	Descriptions	Codes	Quantities	Prices	Whole products
With only DL	83.8	77.8	75.5	73.1	65.1
With rule-based corrections	**84.0**	**90.2**	**89.7**	**87.1**	**78.3**

Table 2: Results in the NielsenIQ dataset for entity tagging using only DL vs adding rule-based corrections.

Experiments for the whole pipeline	f1-score				
	Descriptions	Codes	Quantities	Prices	Whole products
With only DL	65.3	58.9	56.9	54.6	24.2
With rule-based corrections	**65.4**	**69.4**	**69.0**	**66.4**	**35.1**

Table 3: Results in the NielsenIQ dataset for the whole pipeline using only DL vs adding rule-based corrections.

As discussed in Section 3.1.2, we decided to apply an entity tagging schema based on an encoder-decoder built upon Transformers and CNNs. This architecture is inspired by the PICK algorithm described in (Yu et al., 2021). We made this decision supported by the results presented in Table 1, where PICK obtained one of the top performances in the three tested public datasets and using the lowest number of parameters (68M). This trade-off allows to have a high accuracy in DL predictions for entity tagging tasks jointly with light and efficient models. The average f1-score of LayoutLMv3 is the highest one and slightly better than the f1-scores obtained by PICK, but the number of parameters of LayoutLMv3 is almost double (133M). In any case, there is a margin of improvement regarding f1-scores for all the approaches that is expected to be reduced with our rule-based corrections, as will be experimented in the next section.

4.2.2 Whole KIE Pipeline Results

In these final experiments, we use the described NielsenIQ dataset for evaluating the improvements provided by our rule-based corrections with respect to the baseline DL predictions in KIE for purchase documents.

In Table 2, we present results for entity tagging including product descriptions, codes, quantities and prices. Besides, we also add a field named whole products, where a true positive represents a detected product with all its tags perfectly predicted. As can be seen, the rule-based corrections increase the performance of the mainly corrected tags, with an improvement in f1-score of about 13-14 points for codes, quantities and prices. These results clearly demonstrate how the combination of DL and rule-based approaches provides a higher performance in KIE for purchase documents.

With the aim of fully validating our proposal, we also present results for our whole pipeline in Table 3. This experiment includes f1-scores not only based on entity tagging, but also on OCR and product line grouping. We can see a general decrease in performance with respect to Table 2, especially because of the more restrictive metrics calculated in this case. In particular, OCR predictions must be fully matched with the ground-truth word to consider a true positive jointly with the rest of conditions, so low quality images are greatly affected by these errors. Then, we can appreciate other challenges in performance related to KIE apart from entity tagging. In any case, the results for the whole pipeline shown in Table 3 demonstrate again the improvements provided by rule-based corrections with respect to baseline DL predictions.

5 Conclusions and Future Work

The DL era has provided outstanding tools to solve complex problems in fields such as NLP and CV. Unfortunately, generalization and scalability to different use cases are still an open challenge.

In KIE for purchase documents, DL results can be degraded in cases associated with complex formats, low resolution or multilingual scenarios, among others. However, we have demostrated how rule-based corrections can complement DL architectures to enhance the performance of document decoding in the most difficult scenarios.

We have presented a basic set of rules based on business knowledge for correcting some common purchase tags, but more general rules could be explored in the future. Besides, further works could also include confidences application to rule-based corrections or similar post-processing rules for improving other KIE tasks such as OCR extraction.

References

Nadeem Anwar, Tauseef Khan, and Ayatullah Faruk Mollah. 2022. Text Detection from Scene and Born Images: How Good is Tesseract? *Recent Trends in Communication and Intelligent Systems. Algorithms for Intelligent Systems, Springer*, pages 115–122.

Roberto Arroyo, Sergio Alvarez, Aitor Aller, Luis M. Bergasa, and Miguel E. Ortiz. 2022. Fine-tuning your answers: a bag of tricks for improving VQA models. *Multimedia Tools And Applications (MTAP), Springer*, pages 1–25.

Roberto Arroyo, David Jimenez-Cabello, and Javier Martinez-Cebrian. 2020. Multi-label classification of promotions in digital leaflets using textual and visual information. In *Workshop on NLP in E-Commerce (EComNLP). International Conference on Computational Linguistics (COLING)*, pages 11–20.

Roberto Arroyo, Javier Tovar, Francisco J. Delgado, Emilio J. Almazan, Diego G. Serrador, and Antonio Hurtado. 2019. Integration of Text-Maps in CNNs for Region Detection among Different Textual Categories. In *Workshop on Language and Vision. Conference on Computer Vision and Pattern Recognition (CVPR)*, pages 1–4.

Manuel Carbonell, Pau Riba, Mauricio Villegas, Alicia Fornes, and Josep Llados. 2021. Named Entity Recognition and Relation Extraction with Graph Neural Networks in Semi Structured Documents. In *International Conference on Pattern Recognition (ICPR)*, pages 9622–9627.

Jacob Devlin, Ming-Wei Chang, Kenton Lee, and Kristina Toutanova. 2018. BERT: Pre-training of Deep Bidirectional Transformers for Language Understanding. In *Conference of the North American Chapter of the Association for Computational Linguistics (NAACL-HLT)*, pages 4171–4186.

Kaiming He, Xiangyu Zhang, Shaoqing Ren, and Jian Sun. 2016. Deep Residual Learning for Image Recognition. In *Conference on Computer Vision and Pattern Recognition (CVPR)*, pages 770–778.

Thomas Hegghammer. 2022. OCR with Tesseract, Amazon Textract, and Google Document AI: a benchmarking experiment. *Journal of Computational Social Science, Springer*, pages 861–882.

Teakgyu Hong, Donghyun Kim, Mingi Ji, Wonseok Hwang, Daehyun Nam, and Sungrae Park. 2022. BROS: A Pre-Trained Language Model Focusing on Text and Layout for Better Key Information Extraction from Documents. In *AAAI Conference on Artificial Intelligence (AAAI)*, pages 1–9.

Yupan Huang, Tengchao Lv, Lei Cui, Yutong Lu, and Furu Wei. 2022. LayoutLMv3: Pre-training for Document AI with Unified Text and Image Masking. *arXiv:2204.08387*, pages 1–11.

Zheng Huang, Kai Chen, Jianhua He, Xiang Bai, Dimosthenis Karatzas, Shjian Lu, and C.V. Jawahar. 2019. ICDAR2019 Competition on Scanned Receipt OCR and Information Extraction. In *International Conference on Document Analysis and Recognition (ICDAR)*, pages 1526–1520.

Wonseok Hwang, Jinyeong Yim, Seunghyun Park, Sohee Yang, and Minjoon Seo. 2021. Spatial Dependency Parsing for Semi-Structured Document Information Extraction. In *International Joint Conference on Natural Language Processing (IJCNLP)*, pages 330–343.

Guillaume Jaume, Hazim Kemal Ekenel, and Jean-Philippe Thiran. 2019. FUNSD: A dataset for form understanding in noisy scanned documents. In *Workshop on Open Services and Tools for Document Analysis. International Conference on Document Analysis and Recognition (ICDAR)*, pages 1–6.

Seunghyun Park, Seung Shin, Bado Lee, Junyeop Lee, Jaeheung Surha, Minjoon Seo, and Hwalsuk Lee. 2019. CORD: A Consolidated Receipt Dataset for Post-OCR Parsing. In *Workshop on Document Intelligence. Conference on Neural Information Processing Systems (NeurIPS)*, pages 1–4.

Shah Rukh Qasim, Hassan Mahmood, and Faisal Shafait. 2019. Rethinking Table Recognition using Graph Neural Networks. In *International Conference on Document Analysis and Recognition (ICDAR)*, pages 142–147.

Ashish Vaswani, Noam Shazeer, Niki Parmar, Jakob Uszkoreit, Llion Jones, Aidan N. Gomez, Lukasz Kaiser, and Illia Polosukhin. 2017. Attention Is All You Need. In *Conference on Neural Information Processing Systems (NeurIPS)*, pages 5998–6008.

Yang Xu, Yiheng Xu, Tengchao Lv, Lei Cui, Furu Wei, Guoxin Wang, Yijuan Lu, Dinei Florencio, Cha Zhang, Wanxiang Che, Min Zhang, and Lidong Zhou. 2021a. LayoutLMv2: Multi-modal Pre-training for Visually-rich Document Understanding. In *International Joint Conference on Natural Language Processing (IJCNLP)*, pages 2579–2591.

Yiheng Xu, Minghao Li, Lei Cui, Shaohan Huang, Furu Wei, and Ming Zhou. 2020. LayoutLM: Pre-training of Text and Layout for Document Image Understanding. In *International Conference on Knowledge Discovery and Data Mining (KDD)*, pages 1192–1200.

Yiheng Xu, Tengchao Lv, Lei Cui, Guoxin Wang, Yijuan Lu, Dinei Florencio, Cha Zhang, and Furu Wei. 2021b. LayoutXLM: Multimodal Pre-training for Multilingual Visually-rich Document Understanding. *arXiv:2104.08836*, pages 1–10.

Wenwen Yu, Ning Lu, Xianbiao Qi, Ping Gong, and Rong Xiao. 2021. PICK: Processing Key Information Extraction from Documents using Improved Graph Learning-Convolutional Networks. In *International Conference on Pattern Recognition (ICPR)*, pages 4363–4370.

Unsupervised Generation of Long-form Technical Questions from Textbook Metadata using Structured Templates

Indrajit Bhattacharya, Subhasish Ghosh, Arpita Kundu, Pratik Saini and **Tapas Nayak**
TCS Research, India
{b.indrajit, g.subhasish, arpita.kundu1, pratik.saini, nayak.tapas}@tcs.com

Abstract

We explore the task of generating long-form technical questions from textbooks. Semi-structured metadata of a textbook — the table of contents and the index — provide rich cues for technical question generation. Existing literature for long-form question generation focuses mostly on reading comprehension assessment, and does not use semi-structured metadata for question generation. We design unsupervised template based algorithms for generating questions based on structural and contextual patterns in the index and ToC. We evaluate our approach on textbooks on diverse subjects and show that our approach generates high quality questions of diverse types. We show that, in comparison, zero-shot question generation using pre-trained LLMs on the same meta-data has much poorer quality.

1 Introduction

We address automated generation of long-form technical questions from textbooks. Such questions can then be used for technical assessments, such as in interviews and examinations. Existing work on long-form question generation mostly focuses on questions for reading comprehension assessment (Dhole and Manning, 2020; Bang et al., 2019; Xiao et al., 2020; Zhao et al., 2018; Back et al., 2021; Cui et al., 2021; Huang et al., 2021).

We observe that textbook metadata — specifically, the index and the table of contents (ToC) — provide rich cues for question generation. Fig.1 and Fig.2 show fragments from the index and the ToC of a textbook on Python. The index structure is hierarchical and often parsed into an subject and a context (e.g. *functions and classes, managing*). The ToC is similarly hierarchical. The main challenge in question generation from unrestricted natural language content is identifying the relevant entity (or entities) and their context. The mentions of some of the relevant entities is often far away from the context, and the context may also use complex linguistic constructs. In contrast, the grammar for the metadata is significantly restricted, thereby simplifying the detection of the entities and contexts. Additionally, their hierarchical structure compactly and completely captures relevant context. In this paper, we focus on automatically generating technical long-form questions using the index and ToC of textbooks. While structured or semi-structured data has been used in NLP tasks such as knowledge graph construction (Suchanek et al., 2007), table-to-text generation (Wang et al., 2020b) and factoid question generation has been explored from knowledge-graphs (Wang et al., 2020a; Han et al., 2022), to the best of our knowledge there is no existing work that uses semi-structured content to generate questions either for technical assessment or for reading comprehension.

We use structural patterns in the index and ToC to design question templates of varying types and complexity, and then use unsupervised regular expression-based algorithms to generate questions by instantiating these templates using index and ToC entries. Template based approaches have been used in question generation from free text, typically with higher precision than deep learning based counterparts, while generating fewer questions (Fabbri et al., 2020; Puzikov and Gurevych, 2018; Yu and Jiang, 2021). However, we are not aware of use of templates over semi-structured content for question generation.

decorators, 983–995, 1053
  call and instance management, 984
  class decorators, 990–992
    coding, 1011–1020
  decorator arguments, 994
    versus function annotations, 1043
  functions and classes, managing, 984, 995
  justification, 985
  type testing with, 1045

Figure 1: Fragment of a Python text-book Index

We apply our approach to generate questions

Proceedings of the 29th International Conference on Computational Linguistic, pages 21–28
October 12–17, 2022.

Figure 2: Fragment of a Python text-book ToC

from multiple textbooks on diverse subjects such as Machine Learning, Java and PL/SQL to demonstrate its generality. Using automated and manual evaluation, we show that the generated questions are complex and diverse while having very high quality. We compare our approach with zero-shot question generation using LLMs, GPT-3 (Brown et al., 2020) and BART (Lewis et al., 2020). We show that these perform poorly in terms of both validity and diversity of the generated questions.

2 Structural Templates for Q.Generation

In this section, we describe our approach for question generation from text-book index and ToC using structural templates. We focus on generating questions that are *answerable from book context.* These have reference answers in the book, which can be used reliably for assessment. Consider the index fragment from Fig.1. WHAT ARE THE BENEFITS OF DECORATORS? and WHAT IS THE RELATION BETWEEN DECORATOR ARGUMENTS AND CLASS DECORATORS? are meaningful questions, but the index provides no evidence that the book contains the answers. In contrast, the index suggests that WHAT ARE CLASS DECORATORS? and WHY DO WE NEED DECORATORS? are answerable from the book. We want to generate the two latter questions but not the first two.

Index Indexes are typically structured as a forest of trees. Our example fragment shows one such tree. It typically mentions one or more root entities (e.g. *decorators*), sometimes with an additional comma separated context (e.g. *libraries, third-party*). Each child entry is about a specific context of the root entity. These may be one or more related entities (*call and instance management*) or attributes and instances (*class decorators*), sometimes with additional connecting context, which maybe a prefix (e.g. *versus function annotations*) or a comma separated suffix (e.g. *functions and classes, managing*). The context may also be about specific tasks involving the root entity (e.g. *coding, type testing with*). This structure may repeat at the third level. We use NLTK to detect the entities as simple or compound noun phrases, and contexts as involving prepositions (IN) and gerunds or present participles (VBG), making use of separator commas when present.

The templates used for generating questions from index entries are summarized in Tab.4 in the Appendix. First, we discuss question templates based on a single index entry containing an entity phrase e, a context c, or both. (a) WHAT IS/ARE e?, if e is present; (b) WHAT IS/ARE c OF e?, if e and c are both present, and c matches the *examples* regex (e.g. example(s)|instance(s) (of)*); (c) WHAT IS/ARE c OF e?, same as above with c matching the *uses* regex (use(s)|usage|application(s) (of)*; (d) WHAT IS/ARE c OF e?, same as above with c matching the *property* regex (part(s)|component(s)|step(s)...(of|for)*).

More interesting templates are those that consider a parent index entry containing entity e_p, and a child entry containing entity e_c and connecting context c. Some are based on simple patterns: (e) HOW DO YOU COMPARE e_p AND e_c?, if c matches the *comparison* regex (vs|versus|compared to|...); (f) WHAT IS THE RELATION BETWEEN e_p AND e_c?, if c is 'and'. We also generate the *uses*, *examples* and *properties* questions for e_p when e_c is absent and c matches the corresponding regex.

Other connecting contexts c specify action sometimes involving one or two child entities e_{c1} and e_{c2} (e.g. *using decorators in functions*). The specific action patterns for c are VBG, VBG IN, VBG e_{c1}, VBG IN e_{c1} and VBG e_{c1} IN e_{c2}. The corresponding question templates are WHAT CAN YOU SAY ABOUT VBG followed by e_p, IN e_p, e_{c1} FOR e_p, IN e_{c1} FOR e_p, and e_{c1} IN e_{c2} FOR e_p, respectively. Though HOW DO YOU VB is a more natural prefix, lemmatization frequently fails to recover the correct base verb from the VBG form.

A frequent pattern for the child context c is ending with preposition (e.g. *debugging with*, *coding of*, *karma configuration for*). The corresponding question template is WHAT CAN YOU SAY ABOUT c e_p? when the token preceding the preposition is VBG, and WHAT IS/ARE c e_p? otherwise.

Any parent entry e that is unused in the main question template, is used to construct a question prefix 'REGARDING e, ' to completely specify the context, (e.g. REGARDING DECORATORS, WHAT ARE CLASS DECORATORS?).

Table of Contents The restricted structure of the index makes detection of entities and contexts simple. The same restriction, however, prevents the templates from drawing upon context to add natural variety to generated questions. In contrast, Fig.2 illustrates that ToC entries are often complex phrases and even complete sentences and questions. However, the grammar is still considerably restricted compared to that for natural language used inside the book. This forms a nice trade-off between ease of detection and naturalness of the expression. The ToC is however much smaller than the index.

ToC entries are of different types: *question* (Q) (e.g. What's a Decorator?), *question phrase* (QP) (e.g. Why Decorators?), *sentence* (S) (containing non-gerund verb) (e.g. Decorators Manage Functions and Classes, Too), *VBG phrase* (VP) (e.g. Using and Defining Decorators), *simple noun phrase* (SNP) (e.g. Class Decorators) and *complex noun phrase* (CNP) (with coordinating conjunctions) (e.g. Things to Remember about Decorators). We detect these types using simple regular expressions involving POS tags and small dictionaries. The templates for the above categories are Q, CAN YOU EXPLAIN QP?, DO YOU THINK S?, WHAT CAN YOU SAY ABOUT VP?, WHAT IS/ARE SNP? and WHAT CAN YOU SAY ABOUT CNP?, respectively. As for the index, we recursively construct the question prefix using remaining parents. The parent e can again be of one of the above types. We construct the prefix based on the parent's type: 'REGARDING e, ' for CNP and QP, 'FOR e, ' for VBG, 'SINCE e, ' for S, and 'e ' for Q, respectively. The templates used for generating questions from ToC entries are summarized in Tab.3 in the Appendix.

3 Experimental Evaluation

In this section, we present experimental evaluation of our question generation approach.

Data: We use text books on diverse subjects — Python (Lutz, 2013), PLSQL (Feuerstein and Pribyl, 2014), Java (Schildt, 2007), Machine Learning (Murphy, 2012) and Deep Learning (Goodfellow et al., 2016). The first two have the richest metadata structure, with 3-level indexes and ToCs. In contrast, Java has a 2-level index, while ML and DL have 1-level indexes and DL has 2-level ToCs. We process the textbook PDFs to extract their index and ToC automatically. Details are in the appendix.

Deep Models: We compare with two state-of-the-art LLMs. For GPT-3 (Brown et al., 2020), we use its Interview Questions preset. We take BART (Lewis et al., 2020) pre-trained for (factoid) question generation on SQuAD (Rajpurkar et al., 2016), and post-train it for long-form question generation on the MASH-QA dataset (Zhu et al., 2020). This has been previously used for long-form answer extraction. We use contexts and their corresponding questions for post-training. Details of hyperparameter settings are in the appendix. For both models, we split the index and ToC forests into complete individual trees, and provide one tree as one context. For GPT-3, we construct a prompt by concatenating a context with a new line and "Generate interview questions from this book index" (alternatively "book table of contents").

Evaluation: For each approach, we evaluate different aspects of their quality. A question is **(a) context-relevant** if it includes (non-trivial) terms from the context. It is **(b) context-closed** if its non-trivial terms *only* from the context, and only from a *single hierarchy path*. These checks invalidate the two example unanswerable questions at the start of Sec.2. A question is **(c) context-complete**, if it includes non-trivial terms from each ancestor entry in the hierarchy. In Fig.1, a question that just mentions *coding*, without referring to *decorators* and *class decorators* is incomplete. The **(d) level-span** of a question is the number of hierarchy levels that contribute terms to the question. In Fig.1, a question only about *decorators* has level span 1. It increases to 2 by additionally including *class decorators*, and to 3 on further including *coding*. We obtain a question form / template by masking out copied terms from the context. In addition to varying level spans, **(e) the number of unique question forms** is an indicator of diversity of questions. These measures are computed automatically (details in appendix). In addition, we manually evaluate the **(f) validity** of a question by checking its semantic correctness, completeness, and answerability from book context.

Results: The results for Index questions are shown in Tab.1a. Note that the first evaluation is context-relevance. *All other evaluations are performed only on context-relevant questions.* The main pattern is similar across subjects. GPT-3 generates the largest number of questions, but ranks the lowest in context-relevance. It also scores poorly in context-closedness.Structured templates generate fewer questions but with very high quality. BART

Subject	#Entry	Model	#Q.	%Cx-Rel	%Cx-Cmp	%Cx-Cl	%L-Span			#Q.Form	%valid
							1	2	3		
Python	1822	BART	728	96	93	63	94	6	0	10	76
		GPT-3	**6251**	23	72	24	84	15	1	**19**	48
		STemp	1216	**100**	**99**	**100**	50	44	5	15	**80**
Java	2541	BART	1753	81	96	67	97	3	NA	9	86
		GPT-3	**15522**	13	84	28	86	14	NA	**26**	48
		STemp	2294	**100**	**100**	**100**	73	27	NA	11	**96**
DL	585	BART	589	98	**100**	80	100	NA	NA	3	78
		GPT-3	**3943**	44	**100**	18	100	NA	NA	**5**	34
		STemp	556	**100**	**100**	**100**	100	NA	NA	2	**98**

(a) Results for Index Question Generation

Subject	#Entry	Model	#Q.	%Cx-Rel	%Cx-Cmp	%Cx-Cl	%L-Span			#Q.Form	%valid
							1	2	3		
Python	906	BART	42	90	24	45	66	31	3	3	42
		GPT-3	313	92	10	53	76	23	1	16	60
		STemp	**324**	**100**	**100**	**100**	7	33	60	**27**	**72**
Java	866	BART	33	**100**	39	70	82	18	0	5	57
		GPT-3	486	99	12	77	82	16	2	17	62
		STemp	**503**	100	**100**	**100**	4	45	50	**21**	**72**
DL	184	BART	21	95	60	55	50	50	NA	6	48
		GPT-3	**175**	85	19	74	92	8	NA	10	68
		STemp	122	**100**	**100**	**100**	11	88	NA	**11**	**84**

(b) Results for ToC Question Generation

Table 1: Question generation results for BART, GPT-3 and Structural template (STemp) for different subjects. #Entry: no. of index/ToC entries, #Q: no. of questions, %Cx-Rel: pct. of context-related, %Cx-Cmp: pct. of context-complete, %Cx-Cl: pct. of context-closed, %L-span: 1, 2, 3 pct. of level-span 1, 2, 3, #Q-form: no. of unique question forms, and %valid: pct. of manually verified valid questions. All columns after %Cx-Rel are evaluated only for context-relevant questions. %L-span is NA when data has fewer than that number of levels.

generates the fewest number of questions but with higher quality than GPT-3. However, BART and GPT-3 questions are largely restricted to single entries and do not span 2 or 3 levels. GPT-3 however has more variety in question forms.

The results for ToC questions are in Tab.1b. First, we note that here GPT-3 and structured templates (STemp) generate similar number of questions, while BART generates very few. All three approaches mostly generate context-relevant questions. Context-closedness increases for BART and GPT-3 compared to index questions, but is still significantly lower than templates. Context-completeness on the other hand drops for these two approaches compared to index. In terms of level span, BART and GPT-3 questions are again mostly restricted to single entries while templates make use of multiple levels. BART has very few question forms, while those for GPT-3 and templates is similar and higher.

Additional results for PL/SQL and Machine Learning are included in the appendix.

The measures discussed so far are automated. We also performed human validation for all subjects on 50 randomly sampled questions from each of the three approaches, *after filtering out context-irrelevant questions*. For index questions, structured templates have very high validity. BART performance is acceptable, but majority of GPT-3 questions are invalid. The situation is different for ToC questions. While template questions have the highest validity, it is much lower than for index. The performance of GPT-3 increases significantly while that of BART falls close to or below 50%.

Error Analysis: In validity evaluation, the reduced performance of STemp for ToC is largely due to errors in type classification of entries. Unsurprisingly, POS pattern based classification misfires more often for ToC entries than index entries. For example, the ToC entry *Bayesian inference when σ^2 is unknown?* is misclassified as Sentence(S), instead of *Complex Noun Phrase(CNP)*. As a result, the question is generated using the DO YOU THINK template for S instead of the WHAT CAN YOU SAY ABOUT template for CNP.

GPT-3 and BART errors are largely due to introduction of additional irrelevant terms. This happens more for GPT-3 for shorter index entries, as it fails to understand the context. As examples, from the context *wake-sleep algorithm*, GPT-3 generates the question WHAT ARE COMMON SLEEP DISORDERS?, and from the context *elif (else if) clause*,

BART generates the question WHAT IS THE ELIF (ELSE IF) CLAUSE IN A CONTRACT?. Surprisingly, BART makes such errors more frequently for longer ToC entries.

Also, unlike GPT-3, BART typically generates a single question per context, which is an index or a ToC tree, even though it is post-trained with multiple questions per context.

4 Conclusions

We have motivated the task of automated technical question generation from semi-structured text-book index and ToC. We have proposed an unsupervised approach based on structured templates that make use of their restricted grammar and hierarchical structure. We have shows using extensive evaluation that this approach performs better according to many different aspects of quality on multiple textbooks on a variety of subjects compared to zero-shot approaches using large language models.

References

Seohyun Back, Akhil Kedia, Sai Chetan Chinthakindi, Haejun Lee, and Jaegul Choo. 2021. Learning to generate questions by learning to recover answer-containing sentences. In *Findings of the ACL-IJCNLP*.

Liu Bang, Zhao Mingjun, Niu Di, Lai Kunfeng, He Yancheng, Wei Haojie, and Xu Yu. 2019. Learning to generate questions by learning what not to generate. In *WWW*.

Tom B. Brown, Benjamin Mann, Nick Ryder, Melanie Subbiah, Jared Kaplan, Prafulla Dhariwal, Arvind Neelakantan, Pranav Shyam, Girish Sastry, Amanda Askell, Sandhini Agarwal, Ariel Herbert-Voss, Gretchen Krueger, T. J. Henighan, Rewon Child, Aditya Ramesh, Daniel M. Ziegler, Jeff Wu, Clemens Winter, Christopher Hesse, Mark Chen, Eric Sigler, Mateusz Litwin, Scott Gray, Benjamin Chess, Jack Clark, Christopher Berner, Sam McCandlish, Alec Radford, Ilya Sutskever, and Dario Amodei. 2020. Language models are few-shot learners. In *NeurIPS*.

Shaobo Cui, Xintong Bao, Xinxing Zu, Yangyang Guo, Zhongzhou Zhao, Ji Zhang, and Haiqing Chen. 2021. Onestop qamaker: Extract question-answer pairs from text in a one-stop approach. In *ArXiv*.

Kaustubh D. Dhole and Christopher D. Manning. 2020. Syn-qg: Syntactic and shallow semantic rules for question generation. In *ACL*.

Alexander Fabbri, Patrick Ng, Zhiguo Wang, Ramesh Nallapati, and Bing Xiang. 2020. Template-based question generation from retrieved sentences for improved unsupervised question answering. In *ACL*.

Steven Feuerstein and Bill Pribyl. 2014. *Oracle PL/SQL Programming*. O'Reilly, CA, USA.

Ian Goodfellow, Yoshua Bengio, and Aaron Courville. 2016. *Deep Learning*. MIT Press. `http://www.deeplearningbook.org`.

Kelvin Han, Thiago Castro Ferreira, and Claire Gardent. 2022. Generating questions from wikidata triples. In *LREC*.

Xinting Huang, Jianzhong Qi, Yu Sun, , and Rui Zhang. 2021. Latent reasoning for low-resource question generation. In *ACL*.

Mike Lewis, Yinhan Liu, Naman Goyal, Marjan Ghazvininejad, Abdelrahman Mohamed, Omer Levy, Veselin Stoyanov, and Luke Zettlemoyer. 2020. Bart: Denoising sequence-to-sequence pre-training for natural language generation, translation, and com- prehension. In *ACL*.

Mark Lutz. 2013. *Learning Python*. O'Reilly, CA, USA.

Kevin Patrick Murphy. 2012. *Machine Learning: a Probabilistic Perspective*. MIT Press, Massachusetts, USA.

Yevgeniy Puzikov and Iryna Gurevych. 2018. E2E NLG challenge: Neural models vs. templates. In *INLG*.

Pranav Rajpurkar, Jian Zhang, Konstantin Lopyrev, and Percy Liang. 2016. Squad: 100,000+ questions for machine comprehension of text. In *EMNLP*.

Herbert Schildt. 2007. *Java: The Complete Reference*. McGraw-Hill, NY, USA.

Fabian M. Suchanek, de, and Gerhard Weikum. 2007. Yago: A core of semantic knowledge unifying wordnet and wikipedia. In *WWW*.

Siyuan Wang, Zhongyu Wei, Zhihao Fan, Zengfeng Huang, Weijian Sun, Qi Zhang, and Xuanjing Huang. 2020a. PathQG: Neural question generation from facts. In *EMNLP*.

Zhenyi Wang, Xiaoyang Wang, Bang An, Dong Yu, and Changyou Chen. 2020b. Towards faithful neural table-to-text generation with content-matching constraints. In *ACL*.

Dongling Xiao, Han Zhang, Yukun Li, Yu Sun, Hao Tian, Hua Wu, and Haifeng Wang. 2020. Ernie-gen: An enhanced multi-flow pre-training and fine-tuning framework for natural language generation. In *IJCAI*.

Xiaojing Yu and Anxiao Jiang. 2021. Expanding, retrieving and infilling: Diversifying cross-domain question generation with flexible templates. In *EACL*.

Yao Zhao, Xiaochuan Ni, Yuanyuan Ding, and Qifa Ke. 2018. Paragraph-level neural question generation with maxout pointer and gated self-attention networks. In *EMNLP*.

Ming Zhu, Aman Ahuja, Da-Cheng Juan, Wei Wei, and Chandan K Reddy. 2020. Question answering with long multiple-span answers. In *Findings of the Association for Computational Linguistics: EMNLP*.

A Appendix

A.1 Textbook PDF Processing

We process the textbook PDFs to extract their index and ToC automatically. The task is to extract the entries along with their levels in the hierarchy from the ToC and index of the book PDFs. ToC entries often have different text font and size to represent chapter, sub-chapter headers and different indentation to represent different levels as shown in Fig.2. Index entries mostly have same text font and size but have different indentation to represent the level of hierarchy as shown in Fig.1. We first use **pdfminer library** to extract texts with the metadata such as text sizes, fonts, and text coordinates from the PDFs. Then we write a wrapper on top of pdfminer that uses this metadata to filter out unnecessary parts (e.g. header, footers) from the text and annotate different aspects(e.g. entry, level, page no) of the index and ToC. Books from different publishers have different text size, fonts and coordinates for different elements. So the filtering parameters need to customized to some extent for each book.

A.2 Additional Results

The results for PL/SQL and Machine Learning are shown in Tab.2. The observations for the three models are very similar to those for the 3 subjects in Sec.3.

A.3 Automated Evaluation

Here, we describe our automated evaluation algorithms.

Context-relevance: We first identify non-trivial terms by tokenizing a question using NLTK tokenizer and removing stopwords, wh-words and prepositions using NLTK POS tagger. Then we check for presence of these terms and entries in ToC or index by using stemming and a synonym dictionary. If at least one question term occurs in an entry, then we mark it as context-relevant.

Context-closedness: A question is context-closed if there exists a *hierarchy path* from root to leaf in *a single tree* of the index or ToC that contains *all non-trivial terms* in the question. We first create a set of composite terms from all entries, where a composite term is the longest contiguous sequence of non-trivial terms in an entry. We identify composite terms in a question and map these to some entry (or none) using Rouge-F1 score. We finally check if all composite terms in the question have been mapped, and also mapped to entries in a single hierarchy path.

Context-completeness: After mapping composite terms in a question to a hierarchy path of entries, we check if for each matched entry in the matched entry list, if its parent is also presents in the list. If so, we mark the as context-complete.

Level-span: The level span of a question is the number of distinct entries mapped to it in a hierarchy path.

Question form: To extract the form of a question, we mask all mapped terms in it. The resultant masked string is the question form. Then we count the number of distinct forms in a set of questions. Note that, here we report number of question form on context-closed questions.

A.4 Hyperparameter Settings

We experiment with BART-base (Lewis et al., 2020) model pre-trained on SQuAD (Rajpurkar et al., 2016) and post-train on MASH-QA data (Zhu et al., 2020). All experiments are done on 10GB A100 GPU with 8 CPU cores and 30GB RAM. We use batch size of 8 and train the model for 10 epochs. We optimize the model parameters using Adam optimizer with a learning rate of 0.0001.

For GPT-3, we use the Interview Question preset. We set the temperature parameter to 0 to eliminate randomness and keep the other parameters as default.

A.5 Templates Summary

Templates used for generating questions from hierarchical index and ToC are summarized in Tab. 4 and Tab. 3 respectively.

Subject	#Entry	Model	#Q.	%Cx-Rel	%Cx-Cmp	%Cx-Cl	%L-Span 1	2	3	#Q.Form	%valid
PL/SQL	748	BART	1329	98	92	70	92	8	0	22	74
		GPT-3	**10659**	36	68	32	81	18	1	**44**	46
		STemp	2330	**100**	**99**	**100**	44	51	6	16	**92**
ML	2418	BART	2418	97	**100**	78	**100**	NA	NA	6	80
		GPT-3	**17855**	32	**100**	15	**100**	NA	NA	**17**	20
		STemp	2254	**100**	**100**	**100**	**100**	NA	NA	2	**94**

(a) Additional Results for Index Question Generation

Subject	#Entry	Model	#Q.	%Cx-Rel	%Cx-Cmp	%Cx-Cl	%L-Span 1	2	3	#Q.Form	%valid
PL/SQL	748	BART	31	**100**	35	68	74	26	0	3	39
		GPT-3	329	98	3	74	81	18	1	11	52
		STemp	**357**	**100**	**100**	**100**	4	28	67	**13**	**90**
ML	777	BART	32	**100**	25	72	72	28	0	4	69
		GPT-3	**366**	**100**	9	80	76	23	1	15	68
		STemp	344	**100**	**100**	**100**	5	28	66	**20**	**74**

(b) Additional Results for ToC Question Generation

Table 2: Question generation results for BART, GPT-3 and Structural template for different subjects. #Entry: no. of index/ToC entries, #Q: no. of questions, %Cx-Rel: pct. of context-related, %Cx-Cmp: pct. of context-complete, %Cx-Cl: pct. of context-closed, %L-span: 1, 2, 3 pct. of level-span 1, 2, 3, #Q-form: no. of unique question forms, and %valid: pct. of manually verified valid questions. All columns after %Cx-Rel are evaluated only for context-relevant questions. %L-span is NA when data has fewer than that number of levels.

Entry Types	**Example Entry**	**Template**	**Example**
Question (Q)	*What's a Decorator?*	Q	What's a Decorator?
Question Phrase (QP)	*Why Decorators?*	CAN YOU EXPLAIN QP?	Can you explain why decorators?
Sentence (S)	*Decorators Manage Functions and Classes, Too*	DO YOU THINK S?	Do you think decorators manage functions and classes?
VBG Phrase (VP)	*Managing Functions and Classes*	WHAT CAN YOU SAY ABOUT VP?	What can you say about managing functions and classes?
Simple Noun Phrase (SNP)	*Class Decorators*	WHAT IS/ARE SNP?	What are class decorators?
Complex Noun Phrase (CNP)	*Things to Remember about Decorators*	WHAT CAN YOU SAY ABOUT CNP?	What can you say about things to remember about decorators?

Table 3: Types of ToC entries and templates used for generating questions from these with examples.

	Entry Pattern	Condition	Example Entry	Template	Example
Single	e		*decorators*	WHAT IS/ARE e?	What are decorators?
	e, c or $c\ e$	c matches 'use', 'example', 'property' regex	*decorators, use*	WHAT IS/ARE c OF e?	What are uses of decorators?
Parent Child	Pa: e_p Ch: e_c, c or $c\ e_c$	c matches 'comparison' regex	Pa: *decorators arguments* Ch: *versus function annotations*	HOW DO YOU COMPARE e_p and e_c?	How do you compare decorator arguments and function annotations?
		c matches 'and'	Pa: *decorators arguments* Ch: *and function annotations*	WHAT IS THE RELATION BETWEEN e_p AND e_c?	What is the relation between decorators and class decorators?
	Pa: e_p Ch: c	c matches 'use', 'example', 'property' regex	Pa: *decorators* Ch: *examples*	WHAT IS/ARE c OF e?	What are examples of decorators?
	Pa: e_p Ch: VBG e_{c_1} c_2 e_{c_2}	e_{c_1}, c_2, e_{c_2} = Null	Pa: *decorators* Ch: *Coding*	WHAT CAN YOU SAY ABOUT VBG e_p?	What can you say about coding decorators?
		POS(c_2) = IN e_{c_1}, e_{c_2}= Null	Pa: *decorators* Ch: *type testing with*	WHAT CAN YOU SAY ABOUT VBG IN e_p?	What can you say about type testing with decorators?
		c_2, e_{c_2} = Null	Pa: loops Ch: coding techniques	WHAT CAN YOU SAY ABOUT VBG e_{c_1} FOR e_p?	What can you say about coding techniques for loops?
		e_{c_1} = Null	Pa: *decorators* Ch: *using functions*	WHAT CAN YOU SAY ABOUT VBG e_p IN e_{c_2}?	What can you say about using decorators in functions?
		POS(c_2) = IN	Pa: *performing essential tasks* Ch: *hiding source code of stored programs*	WHAT CAN YOU SAY ABOUT VBG e_{c_1} IN e_{c_2} FOR e_p?	What can you say about hiding source code of stored programs for performing essential tasks?

Table 4: Patterns and templates used for generating questions from index entries with examples. Pa and Ch denote parent and child index entries respectively.

Building Korean Linguistic Resource for NLU Data Generation of Banking App CS Dialog System

Jeongwoo Yoon[♠], **Onyu Park**[♠], **Changhoe Hwang**[♠],
Gwanghoon Yoo[♠], **Eric Laporte**[♡], **Jeesun Nam**[♠]
[♠]DICORA, Hankuk University of Foreign Studies, [♡]Université Gustave Eiffel
{skyjw1211, onyubellapark}@gmail.com, {hch8357, rhkdgns2008}@naver.com,
eric.laporte@univ-eiffel.fr, namjs@hufs.ac.kr

Abstract

Natural language understanding (NLU) is integral to task-oriented dialog systems, but demands a considerable amount of annotated training data to increase the coverage of diverse utterances. In this study, we report the construction of a linguistic resource named FIAD (Financial Annotated Dataset) and its use to generate a Korean annotated training data for NLU in the banking customer service (CS) domain. By an empirical examination of a corpus of banking app reviews, we identified three linguistic patterns occurring in Korean request utterances: TOPIC (ENTITY, FEATURE), EVENT, and DISCOURSE MARKER. We represented them in LGGs (Local Grammar Graphs) to generate annotated data covering diverse intents and entities. To assess the practicality of the resource, we evaluate the performances of DIET-only (Intent: 0.91 /Topic [entity+feature]: 0.83), DIET+ HANBERT (I:0.94/T:0.85), DIET+ KoBERT (I:0.94/T:0.86), and DIET+ KorBERT (I:0.95/T:0.84) models trained on FIAD-generated data to extract various types of semantic items.

1 Introduction

Task-oriented dialogue (TOD) systems are rapidly growing in high demand among various industries seeking ways of improving service quality and coping with customers effectively. TOD systems primarily focus on helping users achieve specific purposes such as hotel accommodation, food order, and product recommendation. Natural Language Understanding (NLU) technology plays a critical role in TOD systems: it helps understanding the information conveyed by user utterances, classifying the intents and filling their slots. For example, in the utterance 카카오 뱅크 계좌 개설해 줘 (*khakhao payngkhu kyeycwa kayselhay cwe*) 'Create a Kakao bank account,' an NLU model has to classify the user's intent as 'request for creating a bank account', but also recognize the argument with the named entity 카카오 뱅크 'Kakao bank', fill it in the 'Bank Entity' slot, and identify 'account' as an entity in banking service.

NLU tasks such as intent classification and slot filling are usually implemented by supervised learning, requiring a large amount of annotated training data. However, it is hard to find publicly available Korean training datasets for TOD oriented NLU, due to privacy issues, and constructing them costs considerable time and human labor. In addition, since users produce diverse utterances with different terminologies and linguistic forms depending on domains, annotated training data should reflect that diversity in each domain. The performance of NLU models is likely to be directly affected by this aspect of the training dataset.

Moreover, as most of the user utterances in TOD are meant to request specific information or actions, covering the linguistic patterns that occur in directives and questions is essential to increase the NLU coverage of diverse utterances. In Korean, discourse markers used in requests frequently contain certain patterns with word endings and performative predicates, which can be realized in different moods, e.g. -해 줘/봐(*hay cwe/pwa*). In order to classify Korean request utterances, such discourse expressions should be included in the training data.

This study proposes a linguistic resource named Financial Annotated Dataset (FIAD), which allows for generating annotated training data in the banking CS domain. FIAD specifies linguistic forms with extensive linguistic variations, and has been constructed on the basis of a corpus of

Proceedings of the 29th International Conference on Computational Linguistic, pages 29–37
October 12–17, 2022.

banking app reviews. It consists of three parts: TOPIC(ENTITY, FEATURE), EVENT, and DISCOURSE-MARKER. Each part allows for generating words and multi-word expressions (MWEs) reflecting the characteristics of the corpus in terms of syntax, semantics, and discourse, and contains a meticulous description of their grammatical constraints in Local Grammar Graphs (LGG) (Gross, 1997, 1999). The combinations of the parts allows a generation of training data adjustable to a required size and linguistic characteristics. FIAD covers various types of discourse markers of directives and questions that are challenging for NLU of Korean sentences.

The TOPIC part is comprised of ENTITY and FEATURE. ENTITY covers named entities, and FEATURE includes common nouns related to services. ENTITY and FEATURE are used to fill slots with detailed information.

EVENT covers utterances expressing intents. It invokes modules of TOPIC to generate utterances in compliance with the syntactic and semantic constraints between an intent and the entities or services mentioned in the same utterance.

DISCOURSE-MARKER contains a variety of discourse expressions with predicate endings and auxiliary verbs. This part is largely domain-agnostic. It is modularized according to the Korean honorific system and sentence moods, and covers direct and indirect speech acts.

A main graph specifies how the expressions described in the three parts can be combined into standalone utterances.

FIAD generates named entities and utterances typical of banking apps or services, along with semantic annotations based on the rich linguistic resources. By selecting some of the LGGs, it is possible to generate NLU data of a given size, or tuned to some given politeness levels. It leads to the advantage of obtaining a vast amount of annotated training data containing typical and grammatically fit utterances with time efficiency and less workforce than by collecting or creating the data through crowdsourcing.

Related Work

Building a TOD system for a domain without enough available data resources requires collecting a significant amount of training data and carrying out a laborious annotation process. One of the popular open training datasets for TOD is the Airline Travel Information Systems (ATIS) dataset (Hemphill et al., 1990), which consists of utterances about requests for flight information and which is used for automated airline travel inquiry systems.

The Wizard of Oz (WOZ) and template-based methods are popular for building training data for TOD systems. The WOZ method sets 2 participants: the wizard and the user. The wizard pretends to be a dialogue system, and the user does not know the wizard conversing with them is human. Budzianowski et al. (2018) introduces the Multi-Domain Wizard of OZ dataset (MultiWOZ), which contains 10k dialogues and covers fully annotated conversations spanning over 7 domains. Asri et al. (2017) proposes the ‘Frames’ dataset which contains dialogues about booking a trip based on user requirements.

The template-based method sets a fixed template which consists of entity slots and speech acts-related expressions, and generates data by filling entities in slots of the template. Borhanifard et al. (2020) proposes a Persian dialogue dataset for online shopping dialogue generated by the template-based method. A dialogue system trained by using a mixture of template-based generated data and manually annotated data shows a decent performance. Şimşek and Fensel (2018) presents a template-based method for generating training data. The template structure is based on Web API annotation schema collected from ‘schema.org’.

As for Korean data, C. Hwang et al. (2021) proposes a linguistic resource in the financial technology (fintech) domain. The linguistic resource consists of patterns of queries, complaints and requests in that domain, with fine-grained linguistic information, and it allows for generating and annotating question answering data. The Korea Institute of Science and Technology Information releases a Korean conversation dataset on AiHub (2018)[1]. The dataset covers domains involving small businesses and public services, such as restaurant reservation, online shopping, and public transportation.

However, most of the resources, in particular WOZ-based and template-based, are in English. Resources based on the crowdsourcing method initially contain a lot of noise, requiring several data refinements and complex preprocessing, and

[1] https://aihub.or.kr/

they tend to have fewer linguistic variations, as they are created by random unprofessional contributors.

Local grammar graphs (LGG) have often been devised to recognize semantic categories of expressions, e.g. time adverbs in Korean (Jung, 2005) or proper names in Arabic (Traboulsi, 2006). A local grammar graph is a directed word graph, or finite-state automaton, with paths labeled by linguistic forms. LGG is a powerful method to describe linguistic patterns with lexical, syntactic, and semantic restrictions in a readable way. A graph may invoke subgraphs, which specify parts of the phrases specified by the graph. In other words, a subgraph fills a slot in a graph. A 'local grammar' is usually made up by a collection of graphs.

As opposed to the traditional use of LGGs, which is recognizing phrases in texts, we use them in this research in order to generate linguistic forms. Thus, we implemented a generator of utterances with annotation of slots and intents for a dialogue system. The generator enumerates paths of Local Grammar Graphs (LGGs) and generates large-scale training data covering the Korean honorific system, different grammatical moods, and various speech acts. The generation can be parameterized in order to create training data according to the desired features. Using the training data, we evaluate the performances of DIET models (Bunk et al., 2020) with pre-trained embeddings.

Methodology

FIAD was constructed in three phases: data analysis, resource construction, and data generation, as illustrated in Figure 1.

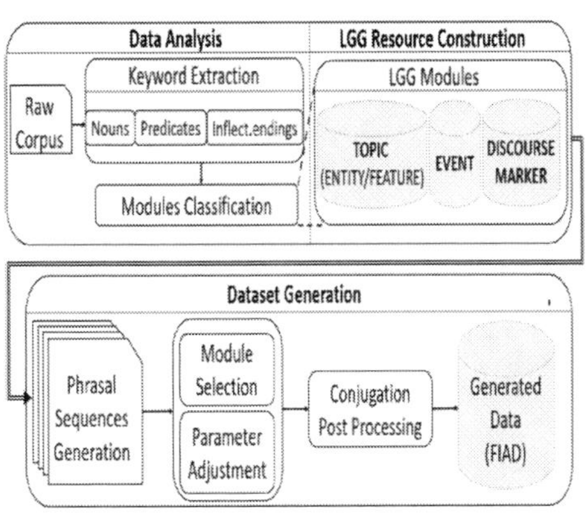

Figure 1: FIAD building process

The first phase, *Data Analysis*, is performed by analyzing domain-specific corpus and extracting core keywords that should be recognized. The second phase, *Resource Construction*, consists of building a Deco-Dom and LGGs that contain TOPIC(ENTITY, FEATURE) words, EVENT expressions and DISCOURSE-MARKERS. Finally, the third phase, *Data Generation*, is conducted by the combination of the three modules of the language resources represented in Phase 2.

2 Data Analysis

Since collecting users' dialogue data raises privacy issues, we collected a corpus of banking app reviews as alternative data. 126,598 banking app reviews were collected from Appstore and Playstore. On a scale of 1 to 5, we focused on reviews with a score of 3 or lower because low score reviews tend to include more users' requests or complaints on banking services than high score reviews.

We used the Mecab-Ko Korean Morphological analyze [2] to split the collected reviews into morphemes. Then, we extracted key morphemes, nouns, predicates, and inflectional endings using their TF-IDF (Term Frequency-Inverse Document Frequency) weight.

Based on the extracted keywords and on the observation of utterance patterns, we set a language resource in three parts: TOPIC(ENTITY, FEATURE), EVENT, and DISCOURSE-MARKER. Each part has submodules which are separated based on their semantic content. All the modules and their sub-modules are organized as shown in Fig. 2. The module/submodule hierarchy means that the expressions specified by the submodule are a subset of those specified by the module. More details on this resource are provided in Section 5.

[2] https://github.com/hephaex/mecab-ko

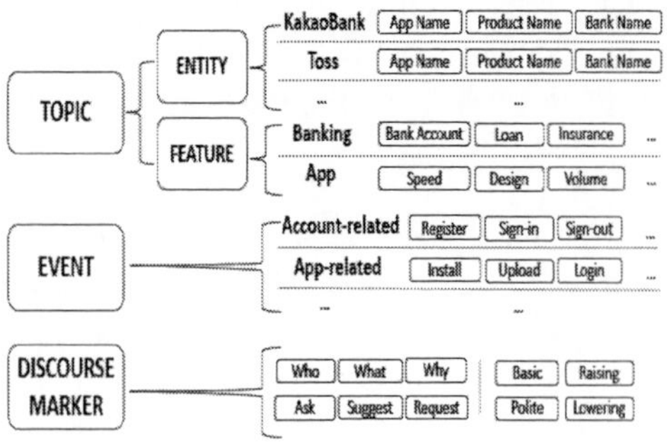

Figure 2: Module and submodule hierarchy

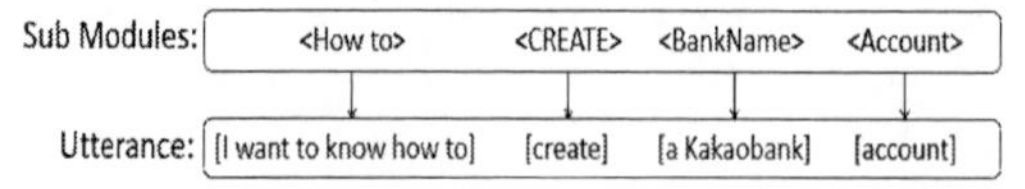

Figure 3: Substituting {ENTITY} Submodules

3 Resource Construction

3.1 TOPIC

We divide the TOPIC part of FIAD into ENTITY and FEATURE for modularity and scalability. ENTITY includes named entities which refer to product names and names of specific banks, and FEATURE includes common nouns frequently used in reviews and dialogues about banking and financial app services. The modules and submodlues of ENTITY and FEATURE are displayed in Tables 1 and 2.

Category	Entity Submodules	# of patterns
BankName	KakaoBank, TossBank, etc.	53
AppName	Kakao Pay, Toss, etc.	167
ProductName	KakaoBank 26Weeks Deposit, TossBank EmergencyFund, etc.	1,938
Total		2,158

Table 1: {ENTITY} modules and submodules

Category	Feature Submodules	# of patterns
Banking	bank account, loan, stock, insurance, etc.	147
App	speed, volume, design, etc.	281
Total		428

Table 2: {FEATURE} modules and submodules

The main role of TOPIC is to fill slots. Modules and submodules of ENTITY and FEATURE are used to set slots in the utterances. This allows researchers to change or add training data of a specific domain by selecting ENTITY modules or submodules, such as banks' product names and bank names. For example, *Kakao bank card* can be replaced with *Toss card* by replacing the <KakaoBank> ENTITY submodule with the <Toss> ENTITY submodule.

3.2 EVENT

We set EVENT submodules on the basis of key verbs from the review data and semantic restrictions on their arguments. EVENT invokes many TOPIC LGGs, due to semantic restrictions, i.e. because verbs in EVENT require a specific type of TOPIC words or phrases.

(1a) <계좌>를 개설하다 (*kyeycwalul kayselhata*)
CREATE a <bank account>

(1b) *<속도>를 개설하다 *(*soktolul kayselhata*)
*CREATE a <velocity>

(1a) and (1b) show an argument-predicate structure with a noun and a verb. (1a) sounds natural, but (1b) doesn't, because the <velocity> semantic category in (1b) does not combine with the Korean verb used in *CREATE a bank account*. We set specific ENTITY submodules whenever an EVENT verb required it, so as to generate natural utterances.

Category	EVENT Submodules	#of patterns
Account	create, sign-in, sign-out, etc.	510
Banking Product	send, take, put, etc.	924
Financial Product	buy, sell, management, etc.	454
App	install, upload, pay, etc.	942
Total		2,830

Table 3: {EVENT} modules & submodules

The modules and submodules in Tables 1 to 3 were established on the basis of a semantic analysis of the topics, events and speech acts expressed in the corpus. In this way, 2,158 ENTITY noun phrases, 428 FEATURE noun phrases and 2,830 EVENT predicative patterns are discerned from the banking App reviews introduced in Section 4. They are representative of the contents of the corpus. This work was performed by speakers of the language trained in semantic analysis.

3.3 DISCOURSE-MARKER

DISCOURSE-MARKER contains various types of multi-word expressions (MWEs) that represent specific speech acts. MWEs are the expressions that consist of several words and connotate specific meanings that can not be derived from their components: ~해줄 수 있나요? (haycwul swu issnayo) '*Could you ~*' is one of the MWE used when speaker wants to request something to hearer.

Request types

In the banking domain, the 'Request' speech act is mainly observed. 'Request' speech acts are further classified in two types: 'Information Request' and 'Action Request'. In this way, the 'Information Request' type is divided into 8 semantic categories, and the 'Action request' type is further divided into 3 categories: 'Dissatisfaction' and 'service error', and 'Demand.' 'Dissatisfaction' and 'Service Error' submodules are not typical types of expressions related to 'Request' speech act, but negative comments to the app and error reportings imply request for fixing bad issues on app functions and services. Expressions of 'Demand' are directly collocated with event phrases, which means 'request for specific action'.

Request type	Semantic category	Example	# of patterns
Information Request	Person	누구 (Who)	2,001,525
	Product	무엇 (What)	1,186,482
	Method	어떻게 (How)	1,401,355
	Reason	왜 (Why)	537,294
	Location	어디서 (Where)	1,872,303
	Time	언제 (When)	510,081
	Age condition	몇살 (What age)	667,860
	Cost/Quantity	얼마 (How much)	322,844
Action Request	Dissatisfaction	짜증 (Annoying)	560,287
	Service Error	에러 (Error)	451,865
	Demand	희망/요구 (Wish)	11,482
Total			9,523,378

Table 4: 'Request types' in DISCOURSE-MARKER module

Sentence types

As an agglutinative language, Korean has a diverse range of inflectional endings with various pragmatic functions: **imperative** endings mainly express imperative 'Request' speech act. However, the 'Request' speech act can also be represented by other sentence types such as **declaratives, interrogatives,** and **suggestives**. Thus, we include four types of discourse endings that represent four sentence types in DISCOURSE-MARKER module as shown in Table 5.

Sentence type	Examples
Declaratives	계좌 개설 [누가 담당하는지 알고 싶어] ([I want to know who is responsible for] creating an account) 계좌 개설[할래] ([I want to] create a bank account)
Imperatives	계좌 개설 [누가 담당하는지 알려줘] ([Tell me who is responsible for] creating an account) 계좌 개설[해라] (Create a bank account)
Interrogatives	계좌 개설 [누가 담당하는지 알 수 있나]? ([Can I ask you who is responsible for] creating an account) 계좌 개설[할 수 있나]? ([Can you] create a bank account)
Suggestives	계좌 개설 [누가 담당하는지 알아보자] ([Let's figure out who is responsible for] creating a bank account) 계좌 개설[하자] ([Let's] create a bank account)

Table 5: Sentence types in DISCOURSE-MARKER module

Honorific types

Korean has various types of honorific markers. The honorific system reflects the hierarchical and relational organization of Korean society and is marked in verbal endings. Korean speakers form their utterances with the honorific levels appropriate to their relationship with the hearer and with the persons they are mentioning. There are three types of honorific markers in Korean: subject, object, and hearer honorific markers. Among these, the hearer honorific markers play an important role in conversations because they refer to the relationship between speaker and hearer.

Korean hearer honorific markers consist of 6 degrees of speech styles: 합쇼체 '*hapsyo*-style', 하오체 '*hao*-style', 하게체 '*hakey*-style', 해라체 '*hayla*-style', 해요체 '*hayyo*-style', and 해체 '*hay*-style.' The first four speech styles depend on the speaker and hearer's social positions and are used in formal speech. The last two speech styles are used in informal speech when the speaker and hearer enjoy some degree of intimacy (National Institute of Korean Language, 2005) .

In contemporary Korean, two speech levels, 하게체 '*hakey*-style', 하오체 '*hao*-style' are being less used. Therefore, we set four categories for Korean hearer honorifics in the discourse marker module. The examples of four types of honorific markers are in Table 6.

Formality	Speech Styles	Category	Examples
Formal	합쇼체 *hapsyo* style	Raising	계좌개설 [누가 담당합니까]? 'Who is responsible for creating an acccount?'
	하오체 *hao* style		계좌개설 [해주십시오] 'Please create an account'
	하게체 *hakey* style	Lowering	계좌개설 [누가 담당하나]? 'Who is responsible for creating an acccount?'
	해라체 *hayla* style		계좌 개설 [해줘라] 'Create an account'
Informal	해요체 *hayyo* style	Polite	계좌개설 [누가 담당해요]? 'Who is responsible for creating an acccount?' 계좌 개설 [해줘요] 'Please create an account'
	해체 *hay* style	Basic	계좌개설 [누가 담당해]? 'Who is responsible for creating an acccount?' 계좌 개설 [해줘] 'create an account'

Table 6: Honorific types in DISCOURSE-MARKER module

The three types represented in Table 4-5-6 are combined together according to lexico-semantic and syntactic restrictions among the elements.

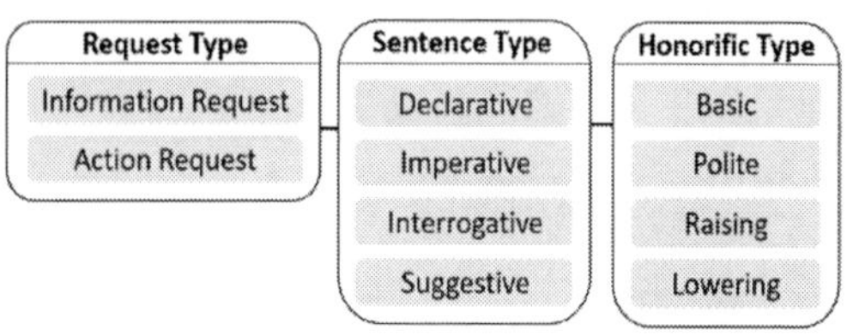

Figure 4: Request/Sentence/Honorific types in DM module

For instance, the combination of '[Information Request]-[Declarative]-[Basic]' generates an example such as '(계좌 개설)하려면 어떻게 해야 하는지 알고싶어. 'I want to know how to do (to create a new account).' and that of '[Action Request]-[Interrogative]-[Raising]' produces an example such as '(계좌 개설)해 주시겠습니까? 'Would you like to (create a new account for me)?'.

4 Data Generation

4.1 FIAD generated by linking-LGGs

We generated utterance data using linking-LGGs with parameter selection and conjugation postprocessing.

Each module of language resources introduced in Section 5 consists of a set of LGGs, which is compiled into Finite-State Transducers (FST) through the open-source Unitex/GramLab platform (Paumier, 2003). The generator outputs linguistic patterns and their annotations by exploring transitions of the FSTs.

The three parts of the language resources are connected in several ways by the linking-LGG displayed at the top of Figure 5. There are four paths in this graph, which represent such combinations: through this processing, about 60 trillion utterance patterns are generated and registered in FIAD. The submodules of each module are used to annotate the 'TOPIC' and 'EVENT' information.

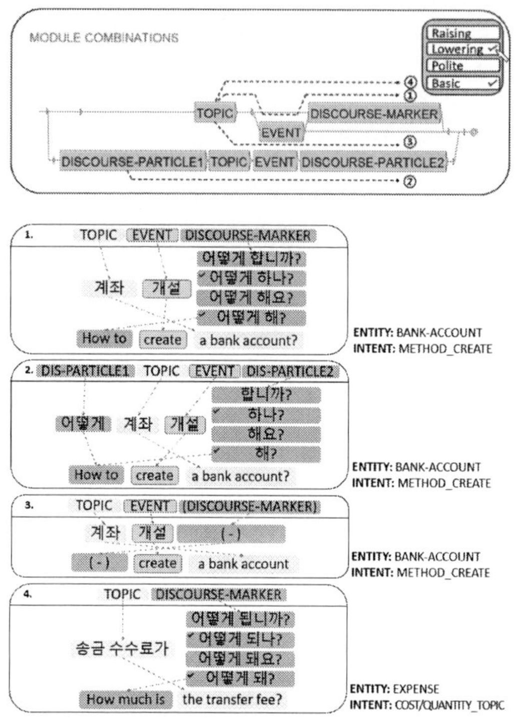

Figure 5: Linking-LGG combining resource modules, and examples of generated results

The first example in Fig. 4 is the basic type of combination, in which TOPIC, EVENT, and DICOURSE-MARKER are connected in sequence.

The second example exhibits a discontinuous discourse marker. As Korean has relatively free word order, parts of discourse expressions, such as 'Wh-words', generated by DISCOURSE-PARTICLE, can occur separately from the rest of the expression.

The third example presents an ellipsis of a dicourse marker. Although DISCOURSE-MARKER is not invoked, the utterance implicitly requests a specific act. Therefore, these utterances are annotated with the 'Request for action.'

The last example shows a case where EVENT is not invoked. The intent of this type of utterance is 'Request for information.'

4.2 Generation of training data

Before the generation of a training data for AI pre-trained language models, we set the speech styles of the utterances by selecting DISCOURSE-MARKER modules depending on the speech styles that the desired TOD system should be able to process. We also set the number of utterances of the training data. We used equation (1) to control the number of utterances. The equation (1) assigns a weight to each expression used in the DISCOURSE-MARKER module, and we generate the utterances with the highest weight to reach the specified size of the training data.

$$w_n = log_2(1 + (syl_{max} - syl_n)) \quad (1)$$

Equation (1) computes the weight of an utterance, which calculates the priorities between utterances. syl_{max} is the maximum length, in syllables, of the expressions in a DISCOURSE-MARKER module. syl_n is the length of the current discourse marker. The formula applies a logarithmic scale to the difference, for normalization. Using this formula, we gives priority to shorter utterances over longer utterances, and this policy is grounded in economy of language. Everyday experience shows that speakers naturally tend to avoid redundancy and use shorter utterances when possible, although this rule is not absolute.

After speech style and data size selection, we generated training data by recursive exploration of the transitions in each LGG module. Since Korean is an agglutinative language, the generation of linguistic forms requires a description of conjugations of verbs. To apply conjugation rules to the verbs, we used the conjugation class information in Dictionnaire Électronique du Coreen (DECO) (Nam, 2018), a Korean lexical database.

5 Experiments

5.1 Comparison with DIET performance

To evaluate FIAD, we used the RASA open source framework [3] and FIAD-generated data to build NLU models that detect and classify intents and entities in utterances. RASA provides a Dual Intent Entity Transformers (DIET) classifier and flexible training pipelines.

We experimented several pipelines to test the performance of NLU models. Each pipeline uses the Open Korean Text Tokenizer (Okt).[4] As to the DIET model, we used the KoRASA hyper-parameters for Korean (M. Hwang et al., 2021), listed under 'DIET-Opt' in Table 7.

Parameter	DIET-Base	DIET-Opt
Epoch	300	500
Transformer layers	2	4
Transformer size	256	256
Connection density	0.2	0.3
Embedding dimension	20	30
Hidden layer size	[256, 128]	[512, 128]

Table 7: Hyperparameters for the DIET-Base and DIET-Opt models

As to the training data, we selected 107 types of intents highly used in the review data. We used 90,999 sequences generated by FIAD with these types of intents.

As to the test data, native speakers created 1,000 TOD utterances about banking CS and annotated the intent and entity slots for each utterance. To compute the scores, we used a weighted average in accordance with the proportions of the intents and the slots. Since there are no comparable datasets with which we can test our dataset, we set the perfomance of DIET classifier with fine-tuned BERT model, trained by NLU-Benchmark dataset (Liu et al. 2019), as a baseline. The baseline result and performance of DIET model with FIAD are illustrated in Table 8.

Model	Tag	Precision	Recall	F1 score
DIET+BERT (Baseline)	Intent	89.67	89.67	89.67
	Entity	**86.78**	84.71	**85.73**
DIET (FIAD)	Intent	**0.9278**	**0.9140**	**0.9142**
	Entity	0.8256	**0.8760**	0.8377

Table 8: Experiment results on FIAD

Although the FIAD is trained without fine-tuned BERT, our model generally outperformed in intent analysis. However, the results showed similar or slightly lower performance in entity analysis: it is due to the TOPIC combinations of ENTITY and FEATURE that raise the complexity of topic recognition.

[3] https://rasa.com

[4] https://github.com/twitter/twitter-korean-text

5.2 Performance of Pretrained Models

In order to check the improvement of the performance, we include pre-trained embeddings in the pipelines. We compared three different Bidirectional Encoder Representations from Transformers (BERT) models for Korean: HanBERT, [5] KoBERT, [6] and KorBERT. [7] These models differ in their vocabulary size and training data. Table 9 shows the result of the evaluation.

Model	Tag	Precision	Recall	F1 score
DIET+HanBERT	Intent	0.9504	0.9440	0.9421
	Entity	0.8465	0.8809	0.8566
DIET+KoBERT	Intent	**0.9616**	0.9510	0.9493
	Entity	0.8506	**0.8952**	**0.8675**
DIET+KorBERT	Intent	0.9613	**0.9530**	**0.9525**
	Entity	**0.8507**	0.8798	0.8486

Table 9: Experiment results on RASA NLU

The 'DIET+KoBERT' model shows the highest f1-score in entity extraction, and 'DIET+KorBERT' shows the highest f1-score in intent extraction. Thus, the experiments underline that the pipelines with pre-trained embedding outperform the pipeline without pre-trained embedding. The results show that FIAD-generated training data allow for training models to efficiently extract intents and entities from utterances.

6 Conclusion

This study presents a linguistic resource named FIAD and its use to efficiently construct NLU training data for Korean banking CS TOD systems. FIAD consists of LGGs and comprises three parts: TOPIC(ENTITY, FEATURE), EVENT, and DISCOURSE-MARKER. Each part contains modules dedicated to semantic categories, and generates utterances where intents and entity slots are annotated as belonging to these semantic categories.

TOPIC(ENTITY, FEATURE) generates expressions used as 'slots' of intents. EVENT provides utterances with an intent and its arguments realized as slots, taking into account semantic restrictions. DISCOURSE-MARKER includes diverse MWEs which represent speech acts, sorted by moods and speech styles, in compliance with the Korean system of honorific markers. These three parts are combined in four ways into four types of utterance patterns for the training data generation.

The models have a clear benefit from the pre-trained embeddings. The performance of the DIET+KorBERT models trained on FIAD-generated data shows 0.86 and 0.95 f1-score in entity and intent extraction, respectively, showing that the concept is applicable. In addition, the modular structure of FIAD offers flexibility for building extensive training data adapted to specific aims, by changing the order of the components or by selecting the modules to focus on particular types of entities, intents or speech styles.

Acknowledgments

This work was partially supported by LINITO Ltd. (http://linito.kr) and DICORA Research Center (http://dicora.kr) in Hankuk University of Foreign Studies. We thank the anonymous reviewers for their helpful comments.

References

Zeinab Borhanifard, Hossein Basafa, Seyedeh Zahra Razavi, and Heshaam Faili. 2020. Persian Language Understanding in Task-Oriented Dialogue System for Online Shopping. In *Proceedings of IKT, the 11th International Conference on Information and Knowledge Technology*, pages 79-84.

Paweł Budzianowski, Tsung-Hsien Wen, Bo-Hsiang Tseng, Iñigo Casanueva, Stefan Ultes, Osman Ramadan, and Milica Gašić. 2018. MultiWOZ - A Large-Scale Multi-Domain Wizard-of-Oz Dataset for Task-Oriented Dialogue Modelling. In *Proceedings of the 2018 Conference on Empirical Methods in Natural Language Processing*, pages 5016–5026, Brussels, Belgium. Association for Computational Linguistics.

Tanja Bunk, Daksh Varshneya, Vladimir Vlasov, and Alan Nichol. 2020. *DIET: Lightweight Language Understanding for Dialogue Systems*. ArXiv, abs/2004.09936.

Layla El Asri, Hannes Schulz, Shikhar Sharma, Jeremie Zumer, Justin Harris, Emery Fine, Rahul Mehrotra, and Kaheer Suleman. 2017. Frames: a corpus for adding memory to goal-oriented dialogue systems. In *Proceedings of the 18th Annual SIGdial Meeting on Discourse and Dialogue*, pages 207–

[5] https://github.com/monologg/HanBert-Transformers

[6] https://huggingface.co/monologg/kobert/tree/main

[7] https://aiopen.etri.re.kr/service_dataset.php

219, Saarbrücken, Germany, Association for Computational Linguistics.

Maurice Gross. 1997. *The Construction of local grammars.* Finite-State language processing, Roche&Schabes (eds.), MIT Press.

Maurice Gross. 1999. A Bootstrap Method for Constructing Local Grammars. In *Proceedings of the Symposium on Contemporary Mathematics*, University of Belgrade, pages 229–250.

Charles T. Hemphill, John J. Godfrey, and George R. Doddington. (1990). The ATIS Spoken Language Systems Pilot Corpus. In *Proceedings of the workshop on Speech and Natural Language (HLT '90),* pages 96–101, USA. Association for Computational Linguistics,

Changhoe Hwang, Gwanghoon Yoo, and Jeesun Nam. 2021. Construction of Language Resources for Augmenting Intent-annotated Datasets Required for Training Chatbot NLU Models. *Journal of the Language and Information Society*, 44:89–125.

Myeongha Hwang, Jikang Shin, Hojin Seo, Jeong-Seon Im, Hee Cho, and Muhammad Bilal. 2021. KoRASA: Pipeline Optimization for Open-Source Korean Natural Language Understanding Framework Based on Deep Learning. *Journal of the Mobile Information Systems, 1-9.*

Eun-jin Jung. 2005. *Grammaire des adverbes de durée et de date en coréen.* PhD, Université de Marne-la-Vallée.

Xingkun Liu, Arash Eshghi, Pawel Swietojanski, and Verena Rieser. 2019. *Benchmarking natural language understanding services for building conversational agents*. CoRR, abs/1903.05566.

Jeesun Nam. 2018. *An Introduction to a Methodology of Implementing Korean Electronic Dictionaries for Corpus Analysis.* Yeokrak, Seoul

National Institute of Korean Language. *2005. Korean Grammar for Foreigners*. Communication Books. Seoul.

Sébastien Paumier. 2003. *De la reconnaissance de formes linguistiques à l'analyse syntaxique*. Ph.D. theses, Université Paris-Est Marne-la-Vallée, France.

Umutcan Şimşek and Dieter Fensel. 2018. *Intent Generation for Goal-Oriented Dialogue Systems based on Schema.org Annotations*. ArXiv, abs/1807.01292.

Hayssam N. Traboulsi. 2006. *Named Entity Recognition: A Local Grammar-Based Approach.* PhD, University of Surrey.

SSP-Based Construction of Evaluation-Annotated Data for Fine-Grained Aspect-Based Sentiment Analysis

Suwon Choi♠, Shinwoo Kim♠, Changhoe Hwang♠, Gwanghoon Yoo♠, Eric Laporte♡, Jeesun Nam♠

♠DICORA, Hankuk University of Foreign Studies, ♡Université Gustave Eiffel

{soown0607, siinwoo0306}@gmail.com, {hch8357, rhkdgns2008}@naver.com, eric.laporte@univ-eiffel.fr, namjs@hufs.ac.kr

Abstract

We report the construction of a Korean evaluation-annotated corpus, hereafter called 'Evaluation Annotated Dataset (EVAD)', and its use in Aspect-Based Sentiment Analysis (ABSA) extended in order to cover e-commerce reviews containing sentiment and non-sentiment linguistic patterns. The annotation process uses Semi-Automatic Symbolic Propagation (SSP). We built extensive linguistic resources formalized as a Finite-State Transducer (FST) to annotate corpora with detailed ABSA components in the fashion e-commerce domain. The ABSA approach is extended, in order to analyze user opinions more accurately and extract more detailed features of targets, by including aspect values in addition to topics and aspects, and by classifying aspect-value pairs depending whether values are unary, binary, or multiple. For evaluation, the KoBERT and KcBERT models are trained on the annotated dataset, showing robust performances of F1 0.88 and F1 0.90, respectively, on recognition of aspect-value pairs.

1 Introduction

Aspect-Based Sentiment Analysis (ABSA) is a sentiment analysis technique which extracts users' opinions on the basis of opinion quintuples consisting of an entity or target, an aspect, a sentiment value, an opinion holder, and a time (Liu 2012, 2015). Since the opinion holder and time can be identified by meta-information sources such as user ids and content posting time, opinion triples including an entity (e), an aspect (a), and a sentiment value (s) are the main components to be extracted from texts associating a semantic orientation with aspects of a target product or service. For example, in (1), the opinion triple plays a vital role in identifying a user's 'positive' (s) sentiment attributed to the 'design' (a) aspect of a 'jacket' (e) target.

(1) [이 자켓]은 [디자인]이 [괜찮아요]
[i cakheys]un [ticain]i [kwaynchanhayo]
The **design** of **this jacket** is **suitable** for me.
(e:jacket, a:design, s:positive)

However, current ABSA systems face limitations in processing texts with Multi-Word Expressions (MWE). For example, (2) shows a positive opinion about a target 자켓 (*cakheys*) 'jacket' with an MWE 마음에 들어요 (*maumey tuleyo*) 'fit the bill; suitable', literally 'listen in the heart', though none of these words conveys a positive value: the MWE is non-compositional, i.e. it functions as a single word.

(2) [이 자켓]은 [긴] [길이]가 [마음에 들어요]
[i cakheys]un [kin] [kili]ka [maumey tuleyo]
The **longer length** of **this jacket fits the bill**.
(e:jacket, a:length-long, s:positive)

Additionally, traditional ABSA opinion triples fail to handle detailed information related to aspects, especially when it involves non-polar opinion expressions. For instance, the aspect 길이 (*kili*) 'length' has a specific value 길다 (*kilta*) 'long', which has pivotal relevance to fine-grained ABSA, as it explains why the aspect has the polarity expressed in the sentence, but this value qualifies neither as aspect nor as sentiment, since it has no sentiment polarity in itself.

In order to cover detailed information, this study uses aspect-value pairs as an enhancement to ABSA, and describes the Evaluation Annotated Dataset (EVAD), which systematically classifies and formalizes detailed opinion elements in online e-commerce domains. We adapt traditional ABSA opinion triples by adding a level of analysis defined by 'evaluation triples' (ET) (Nam, 2021a), which consist of three components:

Proceedings of the 29th International Conference on Computational Linguistic, pages 38–44
October 12–17, 2022.

topic, **aspect**, and **value**. The **topic** and **aspect** are the target and aspect of traditional e/a/s opinion triples. The **value**, however, is a new element for capturing the value of aspects, no matter whether they are realized in the form of a word or of an MWE.

Either the aspect and value appear together in a complex phrase (i.e. aspect-value pair), as shown in example (2), or the aspect term is simply omitted, so we suggest to consider each aspect-value pair as a single item, and to view an aspect term or a value expression as a particular case of such an item as well. In this way, the value, which can be sentiment-oriented or not, may constitute a complex aspect phrase or a sentiment predicate. In this study, aspect-value pairs are categorized according to their semantic characteristics. The first type, Unary, includes existential predicates such as 있다 (*issa*) 'be present' and 없다 (*epsta*) 'be absent', and the polar orientation depends on which Unary aspect occurs. For instance, an aspect-value pair 방수성이 있다 (*pangswusengi issa*) 'waterproofness is present' expresses a positive polarity.

The second type, Binary, contains aspects with binary value, which may convey sentiment or non-sentiment information such as 길이가 길다 (*kilika kilta*) 'longer length' or 짧지 않다 (*ccalpci anhta*) 'not short'. Differently from the first type, the sentiment orientation is not determined by the aspect-value pair itself. When (2) is analyzed with an ET, an aspect-value pair 긴 길이 (*kin kili*) 'longer length', classified as Binary and undetermined in polarity, appears as a complex aspect. As it is associated with a positive predicate, it is subsequently analyzed as 'e:this jacket, a:length-long, s:length-positive.'

Finally, aspects with more values, such as 색깔이 빨강색이에요 (*saykkkali ppalkangsaykieyyo*) 'the color is red', are classified as Multiple. This type of the aspect-value, undetermined in sentiment orientation, may occur as a complex aspect phrase. When sentiment expressions collocate with it, the detailed information is extracted as an aspect-value pair and a sentiment value.

The main contribution of this study is to test a method to extract more intricate information than traditional ABSA, by annotating information about aspect and value simultaneously, without a separate pairing process. In order to implement the notion of evaluation triple presented above into the actual dataset, we built EVAD through the analysis of a massive online clothing review corpus. To build this resource, we used the Semi-Automatic Symbolic Propagation (SSP) method (Nam, 2021b; Hwang et al., 2021) with Local Grammar Graphs (LGGs) compiled into a Finite-State Transducer (Gross, 1997, 1999) and the Korean lexical databases 'Dictionnaire Électronique du Coréen' (DECO) and 'Deco-Dom' (Nam, 2018), to analyze corpora on the Unitex platform (Paumier, 2003). Figure 1 below presents the overall flow chart for the construction of EVAD.

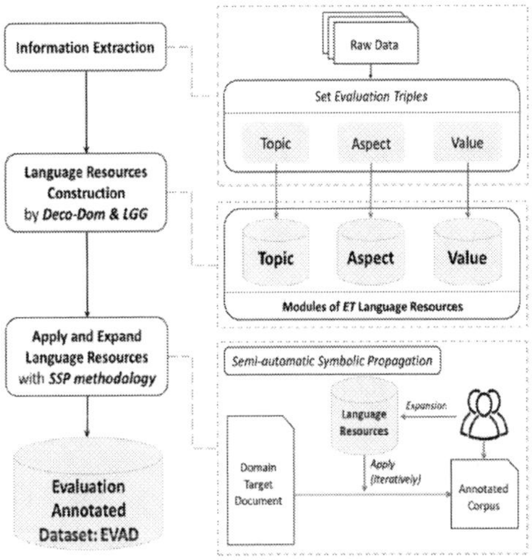

Figure 1: Flow chart for construction of EVAD

2 Related studies

As several deep learning models have been used to perform ABSA, many researchers have developed datasets to train the models.

Jiang et al. (2019) points out that in existing benchmark data, most examples are not significantly different from sentence-level sentiment analysis because they contain only one aspect, or all aspects have the same sentiment polarity. Therefore, the study introduces MAMS, a dataset for more sophisticated ABSA, allowing all examples to contain two or more polarities. The dataset is extracted from the same corpus as the existing benchmark data.

Orbach et al. (2020) notices that existing sentiment analysis studies use data from a limited range of domains, and presents YASO, a dataset from Yelp, Amazon, SST (Socher et al., 2013), and Opinosis (Ganesan et al., 2010) for ABSA learning and evaluation. The YASO dataset covers diverse domains and allows for measuring cross-domain performance. However, it does not provide meta-information on the domains of the reviews.

Other studies define new problems for ABSA. For example, Fan et al. (2019) points out that it is essential to find which words convey the sentiment related to a specific aspect. Therefore, a task called TOWE is defined and a dedicated dataset is provided. Peng et al. (2020) uses TOWE and SemEval data and argues that complete ABSA requires pairing aspects with the corresponding 'opinion terms', i.e. the 'why' expressions that give a clue of why the aspect has the polarity expressed in the sentence, e.g. *friendly* in *waiters/friendly*. These 'opinion terms' describe a value of the aspect.

In some state-of-the-art datasets, expressions denoting aspect values are annotated, but only when they also convey sentiment information by themselves, as in *waiters/friendly*. Our study differs from that practice in that it includes in its subject non-sentiment information about aspect values, when that information is relevant to sentiment analysis.

SSP is a method of generating learning datasets by annotating selected expressions in collected data such as reviews, discussions or questions in the relevant domain in social media. This technology aims to enhance learning data with the aid of sophisticated, large-scale language resources. Once the first dataset is semi-automatically annotated, the language resources are edited based on this first result and applied to the corpus. This bootstrapping approach (Gross, 1999) is applied to the first and second versions of the annotated dataset, producing a third version (Nam, 2021b).

3 Method with Evaluation Triples

In section 3, we propose a method of sentiment analysis that focuses on evaluation triples (ET) and that we have applied to clothing reviews. ETs allow for classifying purchasers' objective or subjective evaluations on aspects such as color, material, pattern..., no matter whether the evaluation is expressed with or without an explicit sentiment polarity. An ET comprises a topic, an aspect, and a value. In the clothing domain, a topic is an evaluation target such as 티셔츠 (*thisyechu*) 'T-shirts' or 바지 (*paci*) 'pants'. An aspect of an evaluation target can be 가격 (*kakyek*) 'price' or 색 (*sayk*) 'color'. A value indicates a purchaser's specific evaluation of a topic or aspect. The main characteristic of ETs compared with traditional ABSA opinion triples is that values include not only single words and MWEs with a sentiment polarity, but also non-sentiment expressions representing purchasers' evaluations about each aspect. Examples of non-sentiment expressions include 길어요 (*kileyo*) 'it is long' and 검정색이에요 (*kemcengsaykieyyo*) 'it is black'. The following sections describe the individual characteristics of each element of ETs in the clothing domain.

3.1 Topics

Topics involve various types of entity names that purchasers evaluate. Table 1 displays the topic classification of the clothing domain. There are five categories. The (CLO_TY) type is the most frequent one, including common nouns of clothing such as 원피스 (*wenphisu*) 'onepiece' and 자켓 (*cakheys*) 'jacket'. The other types are brand names (CLO_BR) such as 나이키 (*naikhi*) 'Nike', online shopping mall names (CLO_SH) such as 지그재그 (*cikucayku*) 'Zigzag', store names (CLO_ST) such as 아뜨랑스 (*attulangsu*) 'Attrangs', and product parts (CLO_PA) such as 단추 (*tanchwu*) 'button'.

Subcategory	Category	Examples
CLO_TY	상품타입 *Sangphwumthaip* (Cloth Type)	원피스, 자켓 등 *wenphisu, cakheys* (onepiece, jacket etc.)
CLO_BR	브랜드명 *Pulayntumyeng* (Brand Name)	나이키, 폴로 등 *naikhi, phollo* (Nike,Polo etc.)
CLO_ST	스토어명 *Suthoemyeng* (Store Name)	아뜨랑스, 리린 등 *attulangsu, lilin* (Attrangs, Leelin etc.)
CLO_SH	쇼핑몰명 *Syophingmolmyeng* (Shopping Mall Name)	지그재그, 서울스토어 등 *cikucayku, sewulsuthoe* (Zigzag, Seoulstore etc.)
CLO_PA	상품일부 *Sangphwumilpwu* (Cloth Part)	단추, 주머니 등 *tanchwu, cwumeni* (button, pocket etc.)

Table 1: Topics in the clothing domain

3.2 Aspect-Value Pairs

An advantage of the ET concept is that aspect and value are considered as paired information, including when the value term occurs without the aspect term. For example, if the predicate 길다 (*kilta*) 'long' appears in the evaluation sentence, this word implicitly includes the aspect 길이 (*kili*) 'length', which can be explicitly realized within the sentence or not, which is more frequent. Therefore, the aspect-value pair is set to save the implicit aspect with a predicate denoting value if no specific aspect is realized in a sentence.

In this study, aspect-value pairs are classified in three types according to their semantic characteristics: Unary, Binary, and Multiple.

First, Unary includes the aspects with values realized in existential predicates. We divide the Unary type into two subtypes: intrinsic properties of the product, such as elasticity and water resistance, and situational properties, such as external properties. Second, Binary is the type for evaluation predicates with binary value, such as 길다 (*kilta*) 'it is long' and 짧다 (*ccalpta*) 'it is short'. Most of such measurement adjectives belong to the Binary type. Third, Multiple is for aspects with more than two values, such as 빨강 (*ppalkang*) 'red', 검정 (*kemceng*) 'black', and 노랑 (*nolang*) 'yellow'. The examples in Table 2 show that sentiment and non-sentiment evaluation for an aspect are considered separately.

Type	Aspect	{ASPECT-VALUE}	Example
UNARY	방수성 *pangswuseng* (Waterproof)	WATERPROOF-GOOD/BAD	방수성 좋은 소재 *pangswuseng coun socay* (It's waterproof material)
BINARY	길이 *Kili* (Length)	LENGTH-LONG/SHORT	기장이 긴 *kicangi kin* (The length is long)
		LENGTH-GOOD/BAD	길이가 적당해요 *kilika cektanghayyo* (The length is appropriate)
MULTIPLE	디자인 *ticain* (Design)	DESIGN-TYPE	브이넥 *uineyk* (V-neck)
		DESIGN-GOOD/BAD	디자인이 예쁜 *ticaini yeyppun* (The design is pretty)

Table 2: Example of {ASPECT-VALUE}

4 Resource construction

We built linguistic resources using the SSP method, which annotates various language patterns in data with the aid of LGGs. We utilized lexical databases (Deco-Dom) to specify the language patterns in LGGs. The main advantage of the SSP methodology is that it produces training data efficiently in terms of time and cost as compared to crowdsourcing, which has been widely used to create large-scale training data. The following sections provide further details.

4.1 Deco-Dom

The Deco-Dom dictionary covers the vocabulary of various domains because users can directly configure it according to the intended purpose or domain. In addition, because it can be configured in a format compatible with the 'Dictionnaire Électronique du Coréen' (DECO) Korean lexical database (Nam, 2018), it enables morphological analysis.

Element category	POS	Examples	Count
TOPIC	noun	자켓, 주머니 (*cakheys, cwumeni*) (jacket, pocket etc.)	1844
ASPECT	noun	길이, 사이즈 (*kili, saicu*) (length, size etc.)	116
VALUE	adjective	크다, 길다 (khuta, kilta) (large, long etc.)	88
	verb	덮다, 맞다 (*Tephta, macta*) (cover, fit etc.)	21

Table 3: Statistics of the Deco-Dom Dictionary

The DECO lexical database has been created through linguistic studies (Nam, 1996), bearing in mind the following methodological safeguards (Gross, 1989):

- grounding decisions on systematic inventories of lexical entries, not on sporadic observations;
- using readable, updatable data formats from the beginning;
- defining modes of inflection (i.e. the set of morphological changes to a lemma when generating inflected forms) explicitly and independently of one another;
- assigning each entry a code for the applicable mode of inflection.

Korean being an agglutinative language, inflection was modularized in two steps (Berlocher et al., 2006), implemented by Paumier (2003):

- generating morpheme-internal morphological variants, e.g. ㅋ (*kh*), a form of 크 (*khu*) 'big', with the method of Wehrli (1985);

- appending suffixes, for instance ㅋ (*kh*) 'big' can be followed by the past suffix -었 (*-e~~o~~ss*), giving 컸 (*khe~~eo~~ss*) 'was big'.

The Deco-Dom is an extension that covers domains by inserting domain-specific tags and entries.

4.2 Local Grammar Graph

Local Grammar Graph(LGG) is a formalism to describe linguistic patterns in the format of directed word graphs (Gross, 1997). LGGs allow for annotating sequences denoting aspect-value pairs. For example, LGGs process collocations such as 뒤꿈치까지 내려와요 (*twikkwumchikkaci naylyewayo*) 'It comes down to the heel' and 짧지 않아요 (*ccalci anayo*) 'It is not short'. Figure 2 shows a part of LGGs that cover the LENGTH-LONG pair.

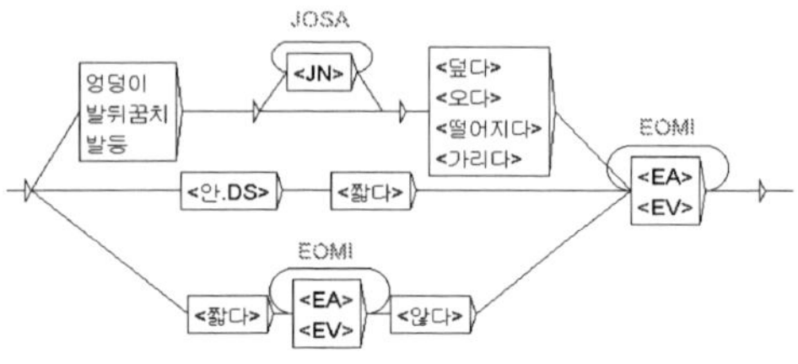

Figure 2: A part of LGGs for LENGTH-LONG

Since an LGG is a directed word graph or finite-state automaton, it is equivalent to a regular expression, but more easily readable and updatable in practice. In its visual form (Fig. 2), it takes advantage of both dimensions: horizontal for sequences of words or phrases, and vertical to enumerate alternatives; whereas a regular expression, in its visual form, linearizes all operations on a single dimension (a formula). Thus, LGGs can describe more complex sets of expressions more clearly.

An LGG can invoke others as subgraphs. This feature allows for managing complexity. As a matter of fact, the above graph is indirectly called by the main graph named ASPECT-VALUE as shown in Figure 3.

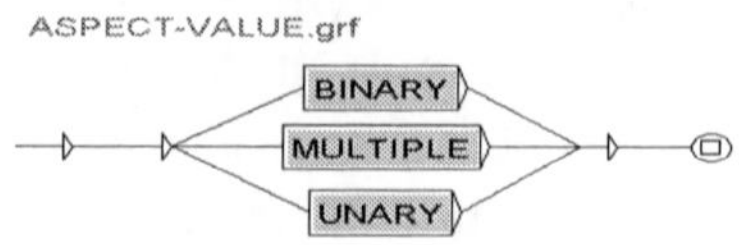

Figure 3: The main LGG for Aspect-Value pairs

Invocations can be recursive, giving LGGs the expressive power of context-free grammars.

LGGs can specify words or word elements either literally, as <짧다> (*ccalpta*) in Fig. 2, or through grammatical symbols, as <JN> which refers to a category of suffix sequences. When the LGGs are used as a query to locate or annotate expressions in texts, the search engine resolves the grammatical symbols on the basis of a lexical database.

The LGG in Figure 3 calls three sets of subgraphs: the subgraph set UNARY which represents 329,153,486 expressions, BINARY with 268,435,457, and the MULTIPLE with 187,856,271 expressions, which allows us to recognize and annotate more than 780 million patterns of aspect-value pairs.

Aspect-Value pair type	# of patterns
UNARY	329,153,486
BINARY	268,435,457
MULTIPLE	187,856,271

Table 4: Number of patterns for 3 types of Aspect-Value pairs

Whe the patterns in Table 4 are detected in a given corpus, the LGGs allow the annotation of the related information through the Unitex platform that compiles LGGs into FSTs for efficient application.

4.3 SSP-based generation of annotated text

The process defined by the SSP(Semi-automatic Symbolic Propagation) methodology mainly consists of two phases [1] : **Human-driven construction** of language resources such as Deco-Dom and LGGs and **Automatic generation** of annotated datasets based on the resources built in the first phase (Nam 2021b).

[1] http://linito.kr/

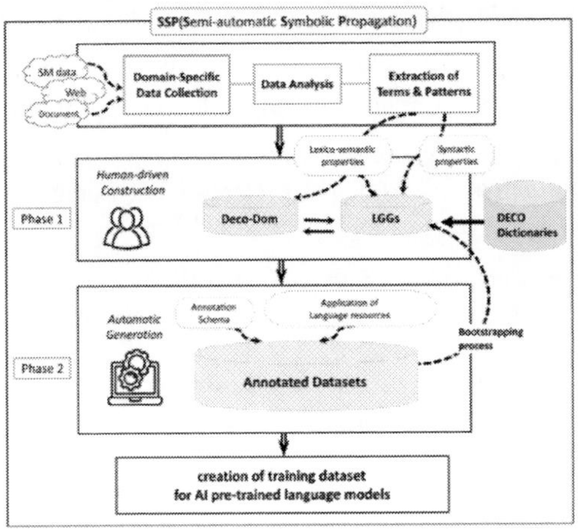

Figure 4: Overview of the SSP methodology

We selected a specific clothing website [2] to collect review data and construct annotated texts. We applied a Deco-LGG resource to approximately 200,000 (199,913) reviews and performed the annotation of the topics and aspect-value pairs through the SSP methodology. Through this processing, we generated evaluation-annotated datasets for fine-grained ABSA. Figure 5 shows examples of EVAD.

<FABRIC-GOOD>재질 괜찮고</FABRIC-GOOD> <SIZE-GOOD>핏이 좋아요</SIZE-GOOD>.

<COLOR-BLACK>블랙으로 샀는데</COLOR-BLACK> <SIZE-GOOD>너무 잘 맞아요</SIZE-GOOD>.

<PRICE-GOOD>저렴하게 잘 샀어요</PRICE-GOOD>.

<ENT=CLO_TY>티셔츠</ENT>는 <LENGTH-SHORT> 기장이 약간 짧네요</LENGTH-SHORT>.

Figure 5: Examples of annotated text sample

ETs in the annotated text EVAD contain detailed information about consumer products. The annotated dataset can be used for a shopping recommendation system which is likely to help consumers make efficient purchase decisions.

5 Evaluation of the EVAD dataset

To evaluate the performance of the EVAD dataset, and indirectly of the SSP method used to generate it, we experimented about aspect-value pairs as they are the core of ET. There are frequent aspect-value pairs appearing in the review corpus, such as SIZE-LARGE, FABRIC-THIN, or PRICE-GOOD. For these categories, we evaluated the annotation of EVAD. We used 1,000 sentences extracted from the clothing reviews, manually annotated them with the correct tags, and evaluated the automatically annotated EVAD sentences by comparing them with the test set. Table 5 displays the results.

	Recall	Precision	F1-Score
EVAD	0.8804	0.8739	0.8772

Table 5: Evaluation of EVAD

The results in Table 5 show that the EVAD datatset, automatically generated through the SSP methodology, reach a F1-Score of 87%.

6 Experiment

We used the KoBERT[3] and KcBERT[4] models in an experiment of training them on EVAD to recognize aspect-value pairs. These models are suitable for this task since they analyze sequences in syllable units. The pre-trained language models KoBERT and KcBERT were used to train the model. Then, the performance of the models was evaluated against the manually annotated test set (1,000 sentences) of Section 5. Table 6 lists the overall performances of the pre-trained language models (PLM).

	Recall	Precision	F1-Score
KoBERT	0.8859	0.8886	0.8873
KcBERT	**0.8990**	**0.9063**	**0.9026**

Table 6: Evaluation of the PLMs

The PLMs show F1-Scores of 88% and 90%, respectively. The reason why KcBERT performance is slightly better than KoBERT is that its pre-trained data comprises informal texts such as news comments.

7 Conclusion

This study proposes an application of the evaluation triple (ET) concept in a clothing domain, and the construction of a linguistic resource, EVAD. The ET consists of three components: topic, aspect, and value. The first two are components of traditional ABSA, whereas

[2] https://wusinsa.musinsa.com

[3] https://github.com/SKTBrain/KoBERT

[4] https://github.com/Beomi/KcBERT

the value is introduced to extract detailed information about aspects. We classify 79 aspect-value pairs described from the clothing domain into three types: Unary, Binary, and Multiple.

EVAD is generated with the SSP method and shows a robust F1-score performance of 90%. SSP-based linguistic resources using an ET frame can be applied to various domains. We expect that the concept and method implemented in this study will be a key asset for research on constructing sophisticated annotated training data for deep learning language models.

Acknowledgments

This work was partially supported by LINITO Ltd. (http://linito.kr) and DICORA Research Center (http://dicora.kr) in Hankuk University of Foreign Studies. We thank the anonymous reviewers for their helpful comments.

References

Ivan Berlocher, Hyun-Gue Huh, Eric Laporte, Jeesun Nam. 2006. Morphological annotation of Korean with Directly Maintainable Resources. *Poster session of LREC*, Genoa, Italy, pp.1803-1806.

Zhifang Fan, Zhen Wu, Xin-Yu Dai, Shujian Huang, and Jiajun Chen. 2019. Target-oriented Opinion Words Extraction with Target-fused Neural Sequence Labeling. In *Proceedings of NAACL*.

Kavita Ganesan, ChengXiang Zhai, and Jiawei Han. 2010. Opinosis: A Graph Based Approach to Abstractive Summarization of Highly Redundant Opinions. In *Proceedings of COLING*.

Maurice Gross. 1989. La construction de dictionnaires électroniques. *Annales des Télécommunications*, 44(1-2), 4-19.

Maurice Gross. 1997. *The Construction of local grammars. Finite-State language processing*, Roche & Schabes (eds.), the MIT Press.

Maurice Gross. 1999. A Bootstrap Method for Constructing Local Grammars. In *Proceedings of the Symposium on Contemporary Mathematics*, University of Belgrade.

Changhoe Hwang, Gwanghoon Yoo, and Jeesun Nam. 2021. Construction of Language Resources for Augmenting Intent-annotated Datasets Required for Training Chatbot NLU Models. *Language & Information Society*, 44, 89-125.

Qingnan Jiang, Lei Chen, Ruifeng Xu, Xiang Ao, and Min Yang. 2019. A Challenge Dataset and Effective Models for Aspect-Based Sentiment Analysis. In *Proceedings of EMNLP*.

Bing Liu. 2012. *Sentiment Analysis and Opinion Mining*. San Rafael: Morgan & Claypool Publishers.

Bing Liu. 2015. *Sentiment Analysis: Mining Opinions, Sentiments, and Emotions*. Cambridge: Cambridge University Press.

Jeesun Nam. 1996. Construction of Korean electronic lexical system DECO, in *Papers in Computational Lexicography (COMPLEX)*, F. Kiefer, G. Kiss, and J. Pajzs (eds), Budapest, Research Institute for Linguistics, Hungarian Academy of Sciences, pp.183-194.

Jeesun Nam. 2018. *An Introduction to a Methodology of Implementing Korean Electronic Dictionaries for Corpus Analysis*. Youkrak Publishing Company, Seoul.

Jeesun Nam. 2021a. *Evaluation-Annotated Datasets Required for Developing Evaluation Analysis-Based E-Commerce Recommendation Chatbots*. DICORA-TR-2021-11, Technical report, DICORA Research Center in HUFS, Seoul.

Jeesun Nam. 2021b. *A Semi-Automatic Symbolic Propagation (SSP) Methodology for Generating Training Data for Aspect-based Sentiment Analysis*. DICORA-TR-2021-10, Technical report, DICORA Research Center in HUFS, Seoul.

Matan Orbach, Orith Toledo-Ronen, Artem Spector, Ranit Aharonov, Yoav Katz, and Noam Slonim. 2020. YASO: A New Benchmark for Targeted Sentiment Analysis. In *Proceedings of CoRR*.

Sébastien Paumier. 2003. *De la reconnaissance des formes linguistiques à l'analyse syntaxique*. Ph.D. thesis, Université Paris-Est Marne-la-Vallée, France.

Haiyun Peng, Lu Xu, Lidong Bing, Fei Huang, Wei Lu, and Luo Si. 2020. Knowing What, How and Why: A Near Complete Solution for Aspect-Based Sentiment Analysis. In *Proceedings of AAAI*.

Richard Socher, Alex Perelygin, Jean Wu, Jason Chuang, Christopher D. Manning, Andrew Ng, and Christopher Potts. 2013. Recursive Deep Models for Semantic Compositionality Over a Sentiment Treebank. In *Proceedings of EMNLP*.

Eric Wehrli. 1985. Design and implementation of a lexical data base. In *Proceedings of EACL*, pp. 146-153

Accelerating Human Authorship of Information Extraction Rules

Dayne Freitag, John Cadigan, John Niekrasz, Robert Sasseen
SRI International
9988 Hibert Street, Suite 203
San Diego, CA 92131 USA
firstname.lastname@sri.com

Abstract

We consider whether machine models can facilitate the human development of rule sets for information extraction. Arguing that rule-based methods possess a speed advantage in the early development of new extraction capabilities, we ask whether this advantage can be increased further through the machine facilitation of common recurring manual operations in the creation of an extraction rule set from scratch. Using a historical rule set, we reconstruct and describe the putative manual operations required to create it. In experiments targeting one key operation—the enumeration of words occurring in particular contexts—we simulate the process of corpus review and word list creation, showing that several simple interventions greatly improve recall as a function of simulated labor.

1 Introduction

To maximize accuracy and robustness under the state of the art in information extraction (IE), one trains machine learning (ML) models, typically underpinned by neural language models, on large numbers of sentence-level annotations (Ma and Hovy, 2016; Zhang et al., 2018; Wadden et al., 2019). If annotations are sufficiently numerous, this approach yields robust extraction capabilities that are difficult to implement through other means. And it has methodological advantages, inasmuch as the annotations serve as a precise extensional definition of a given extraction problem, one that can be trivially exploited in the development of improved extractors through new learning algorithms and architectures.

However, this approach imposes certain costs that are not immediately apparent and that manifest as diminished agility, including:

- *Labor overhead.* Success depends critically on consistent annotation at scale, often requiring a team of trained annotators, the development of clear annotation guidelines, and the employment of a review process.
- *Domain fragility.* The resulting extractors are often domain- or genre-specific, suffering substantial degradation when applied to texts from different, even adjacent, domains. Recent research on domain transfer and few-shot learning offers mitigations (e.g., Huang et al. 2020), but techniques from this research often can only be applied to problems proximal to those for which annotations exist, and often result in models with lower accuracy. Typically, additional annotation is required (Bai et al., 2022).
- *Use case myopia.* These challenges push the IE research community toward problems of putative general utility, such as named entity recognition. To the extent that these "canonical" problems target relatively complex information (e.g., event recognition), they suffer substantial practical limitations. For example, the set of event types encountered in news reporting is practically unbounded, while the types distinguished in canonical resources number in the dozens (LDC, 2005).

Most concerningly, the community's shared focus on a small number of canonical problems, while it fosters replicability and fundamental progress, inhibits progress on methods that would enable the practical deployment of IE on a truly broad range of problems. Many real-world problems involve data or use cases too distinctive to be solved with community models, and many candidate customers of IE lack the resources for adequate data annotation.

Rule-based approaches to IE offer an alternative for the deployment of competent novel extractors (Appelt and Onyshkevych, 1998; Valenzuela-Escárcega et al., 2016). While they suffer from certain limitations—limited retargetability, reduced

Proceedings of the 29th International Conference on Computational Linguistic, pages 45–55
October 12–17, 2022.

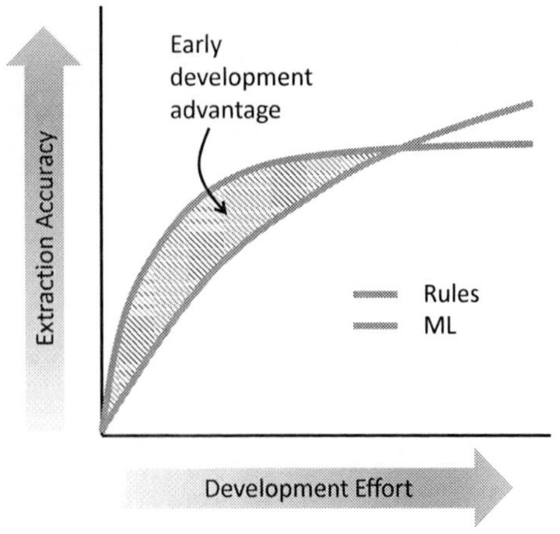

Figure 1: A notional deployment curve comparing the accuracy of rule-based and ML-based extractors as a function of labor investment.

recall, etc.—they possess one significant advantage over ML-based approaches, as illustrated in Figure 1. Specifically, in the early stages of an effort pursuing novel extractors, they support very rapid deployment. Hours of effort often suffice to implement usable extractors, where an equivalent ML-based extractor would require days or weeks. We argue that this "early deployment advantage" makes rule-based IE an important tool in real-world settings. Importantly, rule-based methods and ML are not mutually exclusive. We have previously presented evidence that rule-based extractors can be used to *annotate* training data for ML, and that the resulting models generalize the rules in useful ways (Freitag et al., 2022).

In this paper, we consider a tighter integration between rule-based IE and ML, one in which ML *facilitates* the authorship of rules by offering options and suggestions to the human technician. In a new extraction problem area lacking annotations, the rule author is confronted with a difficult search problem—a difficulty that increases with the expressiveness of the rule language. We hypothesize that ML can be used to simplify the search in ways that dramatically reduce effort. This paper is an attempt to illuminate the dimensions along which such assistance is possible. We approach this through analysis of a historical rule set for extracting quantitative claims from the scientific literature on solar materials. By inspecting how various language features were used in pursuit of a performant extraction model, we attempt to infer some of the operations employed by the author in the initial construction and subsequent refinement of an improving rule set. And we provide preliminary quantitative evidence that some simple interventions could have substantially accelerated a key operation: the creation of problem-specific word lists.

To summarize, we make the following contributions in this paper:

- We introduce the concept of *facilitated rule authorship* for information extraction, a research objective with the potential to dramatically decrease the cost of deploying performant IE on new problems.

- We use a historical extraction rule set to illuminate the operations that human authors employ in their search through the space of possible rule sets. Our intent is to focus attention on human deficits that might be mitigated through focused application of ML.

- We conduct experiments to address one such deficit, the creation of problem-specific word lists, and provide quantitative estimates of the labor savings that can be realized through various approaches to facilitation.

2 Related Work

The use of declarative, efficiently executable rules for information extraction was a common feature of early work in the area, which led to the creation of several rule frameworks (Appelt and Onyshkevych, 1998; Reiss et al., 2008; Thakker et al., 2009). Motivated by the difficulty of purely manual rule creation, early applications of machine learning to the problem sought to facilitate aspects of the authoring process, particularly the creation of what we call *word sets* and what the literature often calls *dictionaries* or *semantic lexicons* (Riloff, 1993; Soderland et al., 1995). This line of research led to some general methods for exploiting syntagmatic search (contextual patterns) for the assembly of paradigmatic resources (lexicons) (Jones et al., 1999), but by treating the lexicon as an end in its own right, it begged the question of ultimate utility for the downstream task of information extraction.

Early successes in lexicon induction gave rise to research pursuing end-to-end extraction through supervised rule or pattern induction (Freitag, 1998; Soderland, 1999; Freitag and Kushmerick, 2000; Califf and Mooney, 2003). This work offered the advantage of improved replicability and retargetability, replacing the highly technical activity of rule creation with the more transparent activity of data annotation. However, once annotated data was available in sufficient volumes, rule-based representations were eventually outperformed by less constrained representations better able to integrate diverse signals in the data (Freitag and McCallum, 1999; Lafferty et al., 2001; Collobert et al., 2011).

The center of gravity in subsequent research has focused on models able to exploit large volumes of annotated data and the acquisition of data in sufficient volumes to realize their advantages. Because annotation overhead hampers application of these methods to new problems, the field continues to investigate approaches to reducing annotation overheads, including few-shot learning (Han et al., 2018; Fritzler et al., 2019; Huang et al., 2020) and transfer learning (Wang et al., 2018; Huang et al., 2018; Yang and Katiyar, 2020). In some cases, these methods make it possible to achieve impressive competence in a new task with very few training examples. But note that such approaches, inasmuch as they often transfer extraction knowledge from known target types or from highly resourced domains to adjacent ones, do not eliminate the need for annotation. And it is often questionable whether the resulting models are sufficiently performant for downstream use without supplementation.

If rule-based approaches to extraction have ceased to be a major research focus, they remain an important tool in the toolkit of practitioners (Chiticariu et al., 2013) and available as features of several general-purpose NLP toolkits (Thakker et al., 2009; Kluegl et al., 2016; Honnibal et al., 2020). Although new rule frameworks occasionally feature in the more recent literature (Chang and Manning, 2014; Valenzuela-Escárcega et al., 2016; Khaitan et al., 2008; Krishnamurthy et al., 2008), these works are almost exclusively descriptive, failing to provide empirical benchmarks that would facilitate continued research in the area. In particular, the process of authoring rules has received no prior empirical scrutiny, making it difficult to corroborate perceived advantages of rule-based methods.

3 A Historical Rule Set

As part of a project attempting to document progress in solar materials research, we developed an extractor for quantatitive "claims," statements that communicated some important scientific mea-

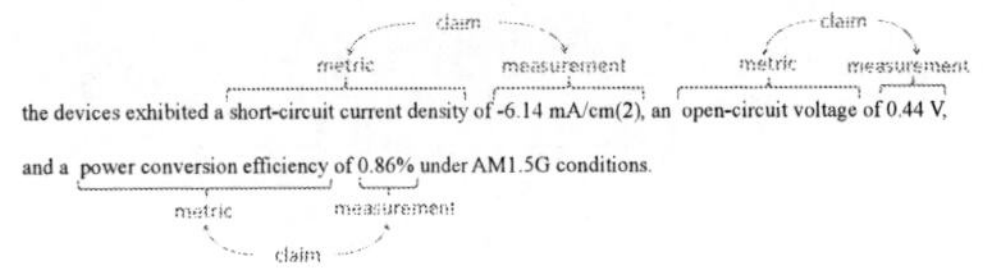

Figure 2: Several examples of the *claim* relation in a sentence from the solar energy literature.

surement. Our experimental data consisted of approximately 160K abstracts from the Web of Science[1] on solar energy research from 1968 to 2014. As is typical in projects like this, IE was not the focus of the effort, but only a means to assemble structured data for downstream analysis, which in this case sought to summarize diachronic progress on several key research dimensions.

As shown in Figure 2, a *claim* is a binary relation between two domain-specific entities or concepts: a quantitative expression or *measurement*, and the corresponding *metric* or quantity being measured. For greatest flexibility in downstream analysis, our definition of *claim* was inclusive, encompassing any expression reflecting the result of a scientific measurement. As the example in the figure illustrates, the two phrasal extraction targets pose different challenges. Measurements, consisting typically of a number and a unit of measurement, exhibit strong orthographic regularities, parts of which could be exploited with regular expressions. Metrics, on the other hand, are noun phrases.

To address this extraction challenge, we employed VALET, a recently described IE rule syntax and framework implemented in python (Freitag et al., 2022). The earlier version of VALET used in this work lacked several of the features of the current framework. In particular, the rule author had no access to syntactic information. Thus, the problem of extraction amounted to scanning tokens in the input stream sequentially, relying on orthographic and lexical clues to decide when the left and right boundaries of the two phrasal targets were observed. We briefly describe VALET's provisions for such scanning to simplify later exposition. Readers interested in more detail or a review of VALET's more recent features are referred to the paper or the more extensive documentation in the public release.

A statement or rule in VALET is a sequence of

[1]https://clarivate.com/webofsciencegroup/solutions/web-of-science/

Type	Example
regex	`/^[a-z]/i`
set	`{ a an the }i`
reference	`&myclass`

Table 1: The types of atomic token class expression available in this study.

three things: a name, a piece of syntax indicatin the type of rule, and an expression defining th rule's behavior. The evaluation of such a statement yields an *extractor*, which can be applied directly to text (e.g., via scripts from the command line) or incorporated into subsequent statements through reference to the rule's name.

The rules in this study relied on two types of expressions, *token class expressions* and *phrase expressions*. The example token class expression

determiner: { a an the }i

defines a case-insensitive extractor matching the individual words listed between the braces. Table 1 lists the full set of atomic token class expressions historically available to the rule author. A full token class expression is a Boolean combinations of these classes using the operators `and`, `or`, and `not`. Thus, the token class

notdet: not &determiner

matches any token that is not a determiner.

Phrase expressions employ a regular expression syntax to match multi-token sequences, enabling the rule author to mix previously defined token classes with literal tokens. In addition, phrase expressions can co-refer, enabling context-free composition. Consider the rules:

```
cap : /^[A-Z]/
honor : { Dr Mr Mrs Ms }
caps -> &cap+
person -> &honor .? @caps
```

The `person` phrasal extractor in this example recognizes person mentions prefixed by an honorific, incorporating a separate phrase extractor for sequences of capitalized tokens (`caps`) by reference. (Unlike in standard character-level regular expressions, the optional '.' has no special significance and matches period tokens in the input literally.)

The rule set used to extract claims consists of 34 rules (15 token class expressions and 19 phrasal

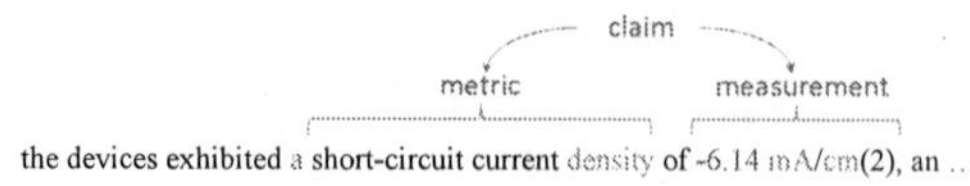


```
claim -> @metric @between @measurement

notmetricword : { . a an the and of to is are … }
metricword    : not &notmetricword
metrichead    : { efficiency voltage density … }
metric        -> metricword* metrichead

quant         -> ( - | + ) ? &num ( . &num )
unit          : { Hz kHz MHz angstrom m nm cal kcal … }
unitphrase    -> &unit ( . ? &unit ) * ( / &unit ) ?
measurement   -> @quant @unitphrase
```

Figure 3: An excerpt of the rule set for extraction quantitative claims.

extractors). We next review the structure of this rule set and consider what it implies about the process of human rule development.

4 Rule Search

A human technician confronting a new extraction problem faces a daunting challenge. Even if they possess the means to observe the effects of any changes to rules, a protracted exploratory process is required to arrive at an effective solution to any extraction problem other than the most trivial. To understand where ML and automation might facilitate that process, we first seek to form an intuition regarding the solution structure for extracting claims, as representative of a broader class of similar problems, then enumerate potential points of intervention in the putative search that produced this solution.

4.1 Rule Set Structure

Figure 3 presents an excerpt from the most productive portion of the claims rule set in simplified form. In this segment, a claim is a `metric` expression separated by intervening language (captured by the `between` rule, not shown in the figure) from a following `measurement`. The key rules implementing `metric` and `measurement` are shown at the bottom of the figure, with coloring to draw attention to how several key components align to the example text.

The phrase highlighted in purple is an example of an extraction constituent exploiting orthographic regularities. The appropriate structure of the numeric portion of a `measurement` follows very predictable patterns and is amenable to succinct characterization. As a consequence, the corresponding rule provides high-recall access to good candidate regions where mentions of `measurement` and `claim` might be found. Such substructures provide a natural starting point at the beginning of rule set construction, providing the technician a means to review a large number of candidate expressions to form initial intuitions about the nature of a given extraction problem.

The rules in green correspond to a very common feature in rule-based extraction models: essentially special-purpose lexicons that list precisely the tokens that may occur in a particular context. Such a feature is critical for the identification of `metric` mentions, which lack the orthographic clues afforded by `measurement` mentions. In this technical domain, the concepts subject to measurement are practically finite, and variations in metric are often indicated through qualifiers prepended to a key head word (e.g., by prepending the phrase "short-circuit current" to "density"). Note that even if the set of possible head words is finite, it need not be small. Thus, if the rule author opts to approach an entity recognition challenge through enumeration, they still face a signficant challenge in many cases.

Finally, the rule in red employs a similar strategy toward a different objective. Specifically, it lists a set of stop words that a `metric` phrase may *not* contain and indirectly defines the start of the phrase as the first word following this boundary class. This objective can be addressed more conveniently through reference to parts of speech—something supported in more recent versions of VALET—but both the problem of delimiting mentions and the strategy of explicit exclusion are relevant in any rule writing endeavor.

4.2 Search Operations

Although we only possess the final product, we are now in a position to infer a plausible sequence of steps by which this rule set was created. Figure 4 depicts such a sequence, with colors to distinguish the various textual regions and classes of operations that were involved. While the actual sequence is unknown, the required activities or operations can be inferred with certainty from the structure of the ultimate rule set. In this section, we describe each of these operations and speculate about opportunities for automation or facilitation.

4.2.1 Anchoring ( )

The starting point for our extraction of claims is the numeric portion of the `measurement`, which,

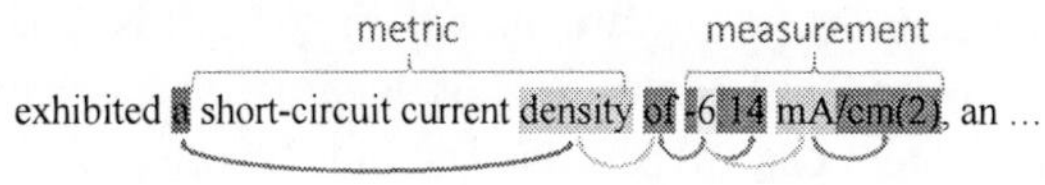

Figure 4: A likely sequence of operations in authoring a rule set to extract claims, including anchoring ( ), elaboration (■), positive word set ( ), and negative word set (■).

as noted, is suggestive of the presence of a claim and largely accessible through surface features. We write a simple rule that matches any numeric token —a rule that overgenerates by design—and use it to inspect `measurement` candidates. Although we show only a single match of this putative rule, it would presumably match multiple spans in the example. However, what matters is that, to a first approximation, this simple rule matches all textual regions in which we might expect a `claim` to appear. Note that this step depends heavily on the technician's intuition and is difficult to automate in settings lacking annotated data.

4.2.2 Elaboration (■)

This syntagmatic operation can be *internal* or *contextual* and involves extension beyond the match boundaries returned by a current rule. In the example, if `6` is the anchoring match, an obvious first step is to elaborate the rule so that it encompasses the entire phrase `-6.14`. Here, we have an early rule that reliably matches tokens or sub-phrases of an extraction target, and we use it to elaborate the *internal* structure of the target.

The interstitial text between measurements and metrics (`of` in this example) provides an example of *contextual* elaboration. We use anchoring numeric expressions to investigate and characterize the "bridge" language that separates our two target entities. If, as is often the case, this language is highly stereotpyical and expressed in a vocabulary of manageable size, we can create a rule for it in a way analagous to our elaboration of the anchoring numeric expression.

The operation of elaboration, which we have defined rather coarsely, almost certainly involves more specific actions that are currently difficult to articulate, but a thought experiment might point the way to forms of machine facilitation possible in the short term. Consider the state of affairs after the initial seed rule and the fact that we match `6` but want a rule matching `-6.14`. Instead of editing the rule directly, the technician might indicate a handful of elaborations, say by dragging their cursor over the complete number phrase in each case, hoping that the system can suggest an accurate elaboration.

The resulting problem resembles grammar induction (Lang et al., 1998), but has some features distinct from the typical framing of that endeavor. For one thing, the examples are embedded, and the surrounding text, which must not be matched by the final rule, provides useful constraint on any proposed "grammar." Second, although the number of ground-truth examples (those touched by the human) may be small, the number of candidate examples can be huge. If the rule author indicates that `6` should be followed by `.14`, we can in principle notice that the pattern *num*`.`*num* is a common theme in the textual regions selected by our anchoring rule. Finally, the induction process has access to a rich and extensible set of elements, as well as a human collaborator to assist in choosing them (or proposing new ones). For example, we have already defined a class of numeric tokens to implement our seed rule, which is available, where appropriate, for characterizing the `14` part of our example expression. Similarly, when we turn our attention to units of measurement, we may define a class that includes both `mA` and `cm`, affording the induction algorithm an easy path to elaborate a rule matching individual unit tokens (e.g., `mA`) to the extended syntax exemplified in the figure (`mA/cm(2)`).

4.2.3 Enumeration (■ and ■)

This paradigmatic operation can be used to address two opposing needs. When we pursue *positive enumeration* (■), we are attempting to specify exactly the set of tokens that may appear in some context in an extraction target, such as the head word of `metric` phrases or possible unit abbreviations in `measurement` phrases (the rules shown in green in Figure 3). In constrast, *negative enumeration* (■) is akin to the definition of stop word lists and can be used to delimit extraction targets, as in the rule shown in red in Figure 3.

In contrast to elaboration, enumeration is a well-defined activity, one that should be readily amenable to machine facilitation. We possess at least two levers that might be used to implement such facilitation. First, if the rule author's approach is to build out from a core component, as in Figure 4, the resulting word sets will be populated with the tokens occurring in proximity to our currently implemented rule set. For example, once we can recognize the numeric portion of a `measurement` accurately, we can tabulate the tokens that tend to follow such expressions (perhaps ranking them by pointwise mutual information with the numeric expression) to derive a noisy word list that can be quickly reviewed and codified in a new token class.

A generalization of this approach, and an approach ultimately offering more flexibility, is to exploit corpus co-occurrence statistics to infer lexical affinities (e.g., through distributional distances or embeddings). Using an authoring framework equipped with such information, a technician might point at a token in context and be presented with a list of semantically comparable tokens, again with the option of selecting some subset to define a new token class.

5 Experiments

5.1 Framing

Our experiments investigate the feasibility and value of automated facilitation of word set enumeration. We simulate a rule author constructing the two word sets shown in green in Figure 3, one for `metric` head words (`metrichead`) and one for units of measurement (`unit`). We investigate two settings. In one, we suppose that before this process begins, the user has created a high-recall anchoring rule that captures some aspect of the context in which the new class of words is expected to appear. In the other setting, there is no such anchor, and the user must rely on other means to find good candidate inclusions.

Unassisted, the user must scan the corpus sequentially, considering candidate words the nominating procedure provides. This is our unit of cost: the review of an individual word for inclusion or exclusion. As each new word is added to the set, our recall of claims improves. Our experiments investigate precisely this trade-off: How can we maximize recall while minimizing human effort? We measure two forms of recall: *word recall*, or the fraction of words found in the respective ground-truth word set; and *claim recall*, the fraction of ground-truth claims found when the current word set is used in place of the ground-truth one. Note that our experiments consider only the situation in which the user has access to some nomination procedure. If a nomination procedure is entirely lacking, labor requirements are presumably higher than any of our experimental alternatives.

For cases where there is no anchoring rule, we must rely on knowledge of the current word set and corpus analysis to suggest additions. For this variant we imagine an iterative setting in which, at each step, the system analyzes the current version of a partial word set and draws on its models of the corpus to present a ranked list of candidate words additions to the user. The user then repeatedly scans down this list until a single good addition is found, then requests a new list. For both of our targets, the initial word set is a singleton containing the first `metric` head word (or `unit`, respectively) encountered in a sequential scan of the corpus.[2]

We experiment with two approaches to unanchored candidate ranking. In each case, we compute a ranking over all terms in the corpus vocabulary that are not in the partial word set and not previously reviewed. The first approach (call it *FT-centroid*) uses FastText embeddings. We rank all possible additions according to their cosine distance from the centroid of the words in the current word set. We also experimented with a variant, *FT-max*, that uses *maximum* cosine similarity. This variant produced results comparable to *FT-centroid*.

The second approach (call it *IT-set*) employs an information-theoretic analysis, where each word in the corpus vocabulary is represented as a distribution over observation contexts. We consider words occurring up to two tokens removed from the reference observation, encoding each unique token and offset as a distinct context (e.g., "`the`" one token to the left is a distinct context from "`the`" two tokens to the right of the reference word). The matrix formed from the set of such distributions is then submitted to a coclustering operation that groups rows and columns while minimizing Shannon information loss. This results in a dense distributional embedding for each word as a distribution over context clusters. We then compute the Hellinger distance between all word pairs and rank all candidate word set additions in descending order by mean distance from words in the current word set.

For anchored review, we introduce the *count* method which simply ranks matches to the anchor rule according to their marginal corpus frequency, suppressing any that the user has already reviewed. To simulate the putative process the historical author followed, we introduce *sequential*, a variant

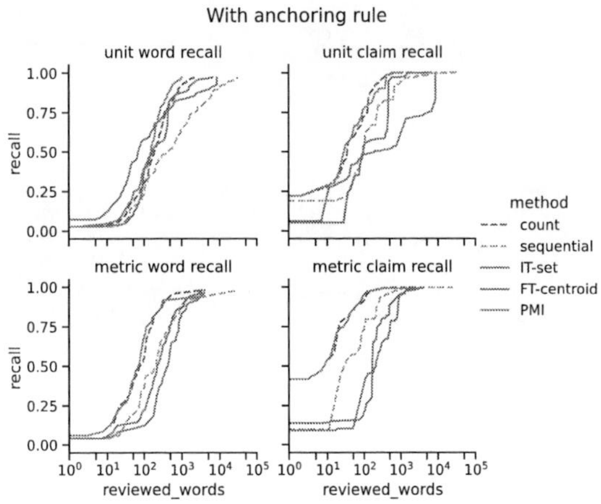

Figure 5: Word and claim recall as a function of words reviewed, using an anchoring rule for nomination.

that considers candidates in corpus order and performs no tracking of already reviewed words. In this case, a word may be reviewed more than once.

Building on the *count* approach, we also explore a point-wise mutual information variant (*PMI*). Instead of ranking by count, we rank by pointwise mutual information between word occurrence and matches of the anchoring rule. This closely follows the counting approach but has extra information about how frequently a word matches the anchoring rule. Finally, we experiment with an anchored variant of the rankers (*IT-set* and *FT-centroid*) that limits their nominations to words proximal to the anchor rule.

5.2 Results

Figure 5 presents results from our experiments employing anchoring rules. In these experiments, the rule used for `unit` nominated any word immediately following a numeric expression. The rule for `metrichead` uses the same numeric expression rule, extended with the rule used to model the intervening text typically found between such expressions and a preceding metric head word (e.g., the word "of" in Figure 3). Obviously, the anchor we use for `metrichead` is more selective than that for `unit`. In the plots, we use a dashed style for *count* and *sequential*, which, because of their simplicity, are useful baselines in both sets of experiments.

As the results make clear, this simplicity does not imply inferior performance. In an outcome that represented something of a surprise for us, corpus-analytic rankers offer benefit to the process of word

[2]This is "temperature" for `metrichead` and "degrees" for `unit`.

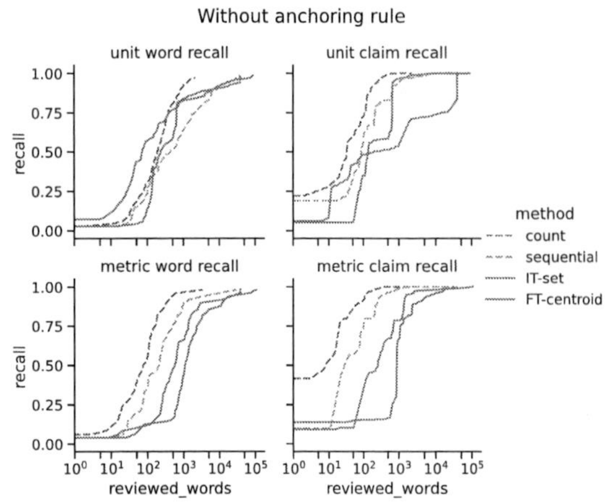

Figure 6: Word and claim recall as a function of words reviewed in the absence of an anchoring rule. The methods *count* and *sequential* do use such a rule and are included in the plot for the sake of comparison.

set enumeration only under limited conditions. In particular, early in the process, *IT-set* apparently nominates more pertinent `unit` words, but the effect disappears as the word set is built out and (crucially) does not apply to claim recall, arguably the more important metric. If the objective is not to find a good set of words alone, but instead to find a set that maximizes extraction recall, it is difficult to improve on a review prioritized by corpus frequency. *PMI* adds incremental benefit in some cases and does not appear to hurt on balance. The key appears to be the selection of a good anchoring rule.

Figure 6 displays the results of our experiments lacking an anchor rule (except for the dashed lines, which are included to make comparison with anchor-based methods easier). Here, *IT-set* continues to display its relative strength on the word recall metric, but the results for claim recall are much more ambiguous. More work is required to resolve this ambiguity, which is relevant to very agile deployment. In cases where reasonable recall is desired as early as possible, we care about, say, the 0.5 or 0.75 recall levels in the plots. Our experiments lead to no clear recommendation for this use case. Presumably, what is required is a variant of these methods that incorporates corpus frequency more prominently into the score used in ranking.

6 Discussion

This work is an initial step in a line of inquiry that could lead to better tooling in support of more agile extraction. The key insight is that once we have a performant rule set, one that we are willing to treat as authoritative, we can simulate the process that led to its creation and experiment with new modes of facilitation in pursuit of greater labor savings and model robustness. Critical to such research, and a focus of future work, is a credible cost model that quantifies levels of authoring effort. Not only would such a model provide a more precise characterization of the "early deployment advantage" of rules over ML, but it could help widen this advantage as an objective function for simulations of the authoring process.

Of course, this approach has certain shortcomings. For one, any model, including our historical rule set, that is not developed and vetted against a thoroughly annotated data sample is typically an approximation, usually one that is recall-limited. In our previous work, we sought to overcome this limitation by using the rule set to generate a large annotated sample to train a high-recall sequence labeler (Freitag et al., 2022). Here, we treat the rules as definitional, but it seems clear that some of the "false positive" elements nominated by our corpus-analytic rankers belong in the definition. For example, only one of the top ten terms nominated for `metrichead` by *IT-set* after two iterations of review was in the historical word set, but many of the excluded nominations appear plausible (e.g., *reflectance*, *oxidation*, or *transmittance*). Many of these words presumably occur rarely (if at all) as part of claim expressions, and our performance metric's emphasis on maximizing recall punishes rankers that promote terms in the tail of the distribution, but a complete account of claim language in this domain might want to include them.

A salient feature of all of these results is our ability to reach full recall quickly using a high-quality anchoring rule and a relatively simple ranking policy. But this outcome may in partly reflect a circularity in the experimental methodology. Our anchoring rules are elements of the historical model, and they therefore necessarily enable us to review all sentences that the rule set considers relevant. A key unanswered question is: what do these anchors miss? Our previous work, which used this rule set to train an ML extractor, yielded apparently valid claim expressions that the rule set does not sanction (Freitag et al., 2022). Perhaps methods such as *IT-set* and *FT-centroid*, which seem wasteful of human effort, can be used to identify alternative or develop more general anchors.

More generally, the structure of a historical rule set is a reflection of the rule language and tooling available to the author, and conclusions drawn from a study of such a rule set may overlook promising points of integration between rule-based methods and machine learning or corpus analytics. For example, the current VALET framework supports on-demand application of *IT-set* via an interactive dialog presenting a large list of words deemed to be close to a chosen word in the text. The user can select any of the words in the list and ask the development UI to generate a new word set expression. Similarly, VALET offers a "radius" statement that matches words within some distance of a seed set in lexical embedding space. And we have begun investigating a trainable word set feature that engages the user in an active learning loop to derive a customized word matcher, one that can in principle exploit contextual embeddings.

While such features are potentially powerful, they sacrifice transparency and fine-grained control–two attractive aspects of rule-based methods. In this respect, they are in the tradition of alternative approaches to rapid IE deployment, such as Snorkel (Ratner et al., 2017), which seeks to learn performant extractors from collections of noisy "labeling functions." Such approaches, for problems on which they work, can lead to impressive labor savings, but they are difficult to control and optimize. But note that while Snorkel-like approaches and traditional rule-based methods approach the IE objective from different angles—Snorkel through redundant, high-recall labelers, rule-based methods through high-precision set covering—they are fundamentally compatible and offer interesting opportunities for hybridization. Trivially, a framework like VALET can be used to conveniently implement labeling functions. By the same token, Snorkel points the way to a mode of rule set application distinct from the typical disjunctive mode.

7 Conclusion

Rule-based methods remain an important component of any toolset addressing the broader problem of information extraction, especially in cases where existing extraction models or sources of annotated data are misaligned to new use cases. A trained technician, outfitted with a suitable rule authoring framework, can create a performant extractor for a new problem in a fraction of the time required to produce a ML model of comparable accuracy. Moreover, we have shown that some simple facilitations, based on an analysis of the rule authoring process, can serve to increase this "early deployment advantage." And by treating rule development as the focus of empirical investigation, we have pointed the way toward future systems in which rules and ML are combined creatively to lower the barrier to entry in the creation of custom extraction solutions.

References

Douglas E. Appelt and Boyan Onyshkevych. 1998. The common pattern specification language. Technical report, SRI International.

Fan Bai, Alan Ritter, and Wei Xu. 2022. Pre-train or Annotate? Domain Adaptation with a Constrained Budget. ArXiv:2109.04711 [cs].

Mary Elaine Califf and Raymond J. Mooney. 2003. Bottom-up relational learning of pattern matching rules for information extraction. *Journal of Machine Learning Research*, 4(Jun):177–210.

Angel X. Chang and Christopher D. Manning. 2014. TokensRegex: Defining cascaded regular expressions over tokens. Technical report, Stanford University Computer Science Department.

Laura Chiticariu, Yunyao Li, and Frederick R. Reiss. 2013. Rule-Based Information Extraction is Dead! Long Live Rule-Based Information Extraction Systems! In *Proceedings of the 2013 Conference on Empirical Methods in Natural Language Processing*, pages 827–832, Seattle, Washington, USA. Association for Computational Linguistics.

Ronan Collobert, Jason Weston, Léon Bottou, Michael Karlen, Koray Kavukcuoglu, and Pavel Kuksa. 2011. Natural language processing (almost) from scratch. *Journal of machine learning research*, 12(ARTICLE):2493–2537.

Dayne Freitag. 1998. Toward general-purpose learning for information extraction. In *36th Annual Meeting of the Association for Computational Linguistics and 17th International Conference on Computational Linguistics, Volume 1*, pages 404–408.

Dayne Freitag, John Cadigan, Robert Saseen, and Paul Kalmar. 2022. VALET: rule-based information extraction for rapid deployment. In *13th Conference on Language Resources and Evaluation (LREC 2022)*.

Dayne Freitag and Nicholas Kushmerick. 2000. Boosted wrapper induction. In *Proceedings of AAAI-2000*.

Dayne Freitag and Andrew McCallum. 1999. Information extraction with hmms and shrinkage. In *Proceedings of the AAAI-99 workshop on machine learning for information extraction*, pages 31–36. Orlando, Florida.

Alexander Fritzler, Varvara Logacheva, and Maksim Kretov. 2019. Few-shot classification in named entity recognition task. In *Proceedings of the 34th ACM/SIGAPP Symposium on Applied Computing*, pages 993–1000.

Xu Han, Hao Zhu, Pengfei Yu, Ziyun Wang, Yuan Yao, Zhiyuan Liu, and Maosong Sun. 2018. Fewrel: A large-scale supervised few-shot relation classification dataset with state-of-the-art evaluation. In *Proceedings of the 2018 Conference on Empirical Methods in Natural Language Processing*, pages 4803–4809.

Matthew Honnibal, Ines Montani, Sofie Van Landeghem, and Adriane Boyd. 2020. spacy: Industrial-strength natural language processing in python.

Jiaxin Huang, Chunyuan Li, Krishan Subudhi, Damien Jose, Shobana Balakrishnan, Weizhu Chen, Baolin Peng, Jianfeng Gao, and Jiawei Han. 2020. Few-shot named entity recognition: A comprehensive study. *arXiv preprint arXiv:2012.14978*.

Lifu Huang, Heng Ji, Kyunghyun Cho, Ido Dagan, Sebastian Riedel, and Clare Voss. 2018. Zero-shot transfer learning for event extraction. In *Proceedings of the 56th Annual Meeting of the Association for Computational Linguistics (Volume 1: Long Papers)*, pages 2160–2170.

Rosie Jones, Andrew McCallum, Kamal Nigam, and Ellen Riloff. 1999. Bootstrapping for text learning tasks. In *IJCAI-99 Workshop on Text Mining: Foundations, Techniques and Applications*.

Sanjeet Khaitan, Ganesh Ramakrishnan, Sachindra Joshi, and Anup Chalamalla. 2008. Rad: A scalable framework for annotator development. In *2008 IEEE 24th International Conference on Data Engineering*, pages 1624–1627. IEEE.

Peter Kluegl, Martin Toepfer, Philip-Daniel Beck, Georg Fette, and Frank Puppe. 2016. UIMA Ruta: Rapid development of rule-based information extraction applications. *Natural Language Engineering*, 22(1):1–40. Publisher: Cambridge University Press.

Rajasekar Krishnamurthy, Yunyao Li, Sriram Raghavan, Frederick Reiss, Shivakumar Vaithyanathan, and Huaiyu Zhu. 2008. SystemT: A System for Declarative Information Extraction. *SIGMOD Record*, 37(4):7.

John Lafferty, Andrew McCallum, and Fernando CN Pereira. 2001. Conditional random fields: Probabilistic models for segmenting and labeling sequence data. In *Proceedings of the Eighteenth International Conference on Machine Learning (ICML)*.

Kevin J. Lang, Barak A. Pearlmutter, and Rodney A. Price. 1998. Results of the Abbadingo one DFA learning competition and a new evidence-driven state merging algorithm. In *Grammatical Inference*, pages 1–12. Springer.

LDC. 2005. *ACE (Automatic Content Extraction) English Annotation Guidelines for Events*. Linguistic Data Consortium.

Xuezhe Ma and Eduard Hovy. 2016. End-to-end sequence labeling via bi-directional lstm-cnns-crf. In *Proceedings of the 54th Annual Meeting of the Association for Computational Linguistics (Volume 1: Long Papers)*, pages 1064–1074.

Alexander J. Ratner, Stephen H. Bach, Henry R. Ehrenberg, and Chris Ré. 2017. Snorkel: Fast training set generation for information extraction. In *Proceedings of the 2017 ACM international conference on management of data*, pages 1683–1686.

Frederick Reiss, Sriram Raghavan, Huaiyu Zhu, Frederick Reiss, Sriram Raghavan, Rajasekar Krishnamurthy, Huaiyu Zhu, and Shivakumar Vaithyanathan. 2008. An algebraic approach to rule-based information extraction. In *In ICDE*, pages 933–942. IEEE.

Ellen Riloff. 1993. Automatically constructing a dictionary for information extraction tasks. In *Proceedings of the Eleventh National Conference on Artificial Intelligence (AAAI)*.

Stephen Soderland. 1999. Learning information extraction rules for semi-structured and free text. *Machine learning*, 34(1):233–272. Publisher: Springer.

Stephen Soderland, David Fisher, Jonathan Aseltine, and Wendy Lehnert. 1995. CRYSTAL: inducing a conceptual dictionary. In *Proceedings of the Fourteenth International Joint Conference on Artificial Intelligence (IJCAI)*.

Dhaval Thakker, Taha Osman, and Phil Lakin. 2009. GATE JAPE grammar tutorial.

Marco A Valenzuela-Escárcega, Gus Hahn-Powell, and Mihai Surdeanu. 2016. Odin's runes: A rule language for information extraction. In *Proceedings of the Tenth International Conference on Language Resources and Evaluation (LREC'16)*, pages 322–329.

David Wadden, Ulme Wennberg, Yi Luan, and Hannaneh Hajishirzi. 2019. Entity, relation, and event extraction with contextualized span representations. In *Proceedings of the 2019 Conference on Empirical Methods in Natural Language Processing and the 9th International Joint Conference on Natural Language Processing (EMNLP-IJCNLP)*, pages 5784–5789.

Zhenghui Wang, Yanru Qu, Liheng Chen, Jian Shen, Weinan Zhang, Shaodian Zhang, Yimei Gao, Gen Gu, Ken Chen, and Yong Yu. 2018. Label-aware double transfer learning for cross-specialty medical named entity recognition. In *Proceedings of the 2018 Conference of the North American Chapter of the Association for Computational Linguistics: Human Language Technologies, Volume 1 (Long Papers)*, pages 1–15.

Yi Yang and Arzoo Katiyar. 2020. Frustratingly simple few-shot named entity recognition with structured nearest neighbor learning. In *Proceedings of the 2020 Conference on Empirical Methods in Natural Language Processing (EMNLP)*, pages 6365–6375.

Yuhao Zhang, Peng Qi, and Christopher D Manning. 2018. Graph convolution over pruned dependency trees improves relation extraction. In *Proceedings of the 2018 Conference on Empirical Methods in Natural Language Processing*, pages 2205–2215.

Syntax-driven Data Augmentation for Named Entity Recognition

Arie Pratama Sutiono
University of Arizona
Linguistics
ariesutiono@arizona.edu

Gus Hahn-Powell
University of Arizona
Linguistics
hahnpowell@arizona.edu

Abstract

In low resource settings, data augmentation strategies are commonly leveraged to improve performance. Numerous approaches have attempted document-level augmentation (e.g., text classification), but few studies have explored token-level augmentation. Performed naively, data augmentation can produce semantically incongruent and ungrammatical examples. In this work, we compare simple masked language model replacement and an augmentation method using constituency tree mutations to improve the performance of named entity recognition in low-resource settings with the aim of preserving linguistic cohesion of the augmented sentences.

1 Introduction

Deep neural networks have proven effective for a wide variety of tasks in natural language processing; however, these networks often require large annotated datasets before they begin to outperform simpler models. Such data is not always available or sufficiently diverse, and its collection and annotation can be an expensive and slow process. The trend of fine-tuning large-scale language models originally trained using self-supervision has helped to alleviate the need for large annotated datasets, but this approach relies on the dataset for fine-tuning being diverse enough to train a model that generalizes well. Careful data augmentation can help to improve dataset diversity and ultimately the model's generalizability.

Data augmentation, a technique to generate data given training set characteristics, continues to play a critical role in low-resource settings; however, the majority of work on data augmentation focuses on improving document-level tasks such as text classification. Far less attention has been paid to token-level tasks (Feng et al., 2021).

Prevailing approaches to sequence tagging tasks such as named entity recognition (NER) require token-level ground truth. Naive replacement-based methods for augmentation may introduce noise in the form of sentences that are ungrammatical, semantically vacuous, or semantically incongruent. Whether in the form of insertions, deletions, or substitutions, care must be taken with token-level augmentation to preserve linguistic cohesion.

There is evidence that large language models may possess some syntactic knowledge (Hewitt and Manning, 2019; Wei et al., 2021). Work by Bai et al. (2021) suggests that incorporating syntactic tasks into pre-training improves the performance of large language models. Inspired by these findings, we investigate how constituency trees might be used to guide data augmentation. We use tree-based transformations to mutate sentences while minimizing undesired side effects of syntactic manipulation (i.e., preserving linguistic cohesion). Related work by Zhang et al. (2022) explores a similar approach in different settings. They focus on the effect of constituency based replacement in single classification and pair sentence classification tasks, while this work examines token-level classification.

We compare our syntax-driven method with no augmentation (our baseline), augmented data generated through cloze-style (Taylor, 1953) masked language modeling using a BERT-based classifier, successful approaches introduced by Dai and Adel (2021), and two of the top-performing augmentation strategies according to past work: synonym-based replacement and mention-based replacement. Following prior work, we We use the i2b2-2010 English language dataset (Uzuner et al., 2011) for NER.

2 Related work

A variety of approaches have been explored for document-level data augmentation. The usage of backtranslation to generate augmented samples was introduced by Kobayashi (2018). Wei and Zou (2019) explored synonym replacement, random in-

Proceedings of the 29th International Conference on Computational Linguistic, pages 56–60
October 12–17, 2022.

sertion, random swap, and random deletion for text classification. Quteineh et al. (2020) introduced an approach using monte carlo tree search (MCTS) to guide generation of synthetic data.

Augmentation for token-level sequence tagging, however, is understudied. Simple approaches for token-level classification (e.g., synonym replacement, mention replacement, shuffling, etc.) was investigated by Devlin et al. (2019). They used a sample of 50, 150, and 500 sentences to simulate a low-resource setting. Token linearization (TL) was introduced by Ding et al. (2020). The main idea of TL is to incorporate NER tags inside the training sentences themselves. Ding et al. (2020) experimented with various sizes of training data across six languages.

A Similar idea to that presented here has been used in parallel research by Zhang et al. (2022). Their approach, TreeMix, works similarly to our approach in that it replaces a phrase with another phrase from another another training instance by swapping phrases with the same constituent labels. Zhang et al. (2022) demonstrated that TreeMix outperforms a method that selects a random span of text as the replacement for a target phrase, suggesting that syntactically=aware replacement can improve data augmentation for at least some tasks.

3 Approach

3.1 Synonym Replacement (SR)

Dai and Adel (2021) experimented with replacing randomly selected tokens from the training corpus with a multiword synonyms originating from WordNet (Miller, 1992). In this case, if the replaced token is the beginning of a mention (B-ENTITY), then the first token of the synonym will be tagged as B-ENTITY and the rest will be considered as I-ENTITY. In cases where the replaced token is in the middle of a mention (I-ENTITY), then all of the synonym's tokens will be assigned to I-ENTITY.

3.2 Mention Replacement (MR)

Dai and Adel (2021) described mention replacement as using a Bernoulli distribution to decide whether each mention should be replaced. If yes, then another mention which has the same entity type as the target mention from the original training set is selected to replace the target mention. For instance, if the mention "myelopathy / B-PROBLEM is selected for replacement, then we can select one of {"C5-6", "COPD", ...} which all have the same entity type (PROBLEM).

3.3 Language Model (LM)

We experimented with token replacement using a masked language model. We restrict the system to replace only non-mention tokens (tokens with category O). This is because if we replace tokens with a named entity, we cannot guarantee that the output from the masked language model will have the same category, such that if we replace a token categorized as B-TEST, we could not guarantee that the masked language model will replace it with a similar token to those in B-TEST category.

We randomly select, without replacement, n tokens as candidates to be replaced. The selected tokens are masked from the original sentence. Next, we the language model generates replacements for the masked tokens. We may repeat this token generation up to k times to generate different augmented sentences. We use Allen AI's SciBERT model from the Hugging Face model repository.

3.4 Constituency Replacement (CR)

As a preprocessing step, we perform constituency parsing over all of the training data using Stanza (Qi et al., 2020). Given an XP non-terminal, we select p non-terminals as candidates for replacement. For each non-terminal, we find other non-terminals with the same category from the training data, to replace the candidate. Assuming that we chose VP as the non-terminal taget node for replacement, the algorithm will choose another VP from the set of parsed sentences in the training corpus and mutate the whole subtree (VP root and the nodes below it). We can repeat this process to generate k augmented sentences. Additionally, we target nodes that have NER mentions as one of its children.

4 Experiments and Results

4.1 Dataset

We used the i2b2-2010 dataset (Uzuner et al., 2011), an English language NER dataset. Similar to Dai and Adel (2021) we use 3 different sizes of dataset to simulate low-resource settings. We select the first 50, 150, and 500 sentences from training set and denote them as S, M, L. We used the default train-test split and limit the augmentations to training set.

4.2 Model

Following Dai and Adel (2021), we model NER task as sequence-labeling. We used same components for modeling: a neural encoder and a conditional random field layer. For our neural encoder, We used SciBERT. This model has been proven to work effectively with scientific and medical data, like i2b2-2010.

4.3 Experiments

Each experiment was repeated with 5 different random seeds to calculate standard deviation.

For our SR and MR approaches, our hyperparameters are the replace ratio (0.3) and the number of generated samples (1).

LM and CR hyperparameters are similar. Both will have the number of generated samples and number of replaced tokens (only for LM) or non-terminals (only for ST). In this work, we limit CR replacements to non-terminals (phrases) in the following set: {NP, VP, ADJP, ADVP, PP}. We leave out FRAG (fragment) because it has too low of a non-terminal count.

One question to be explored is whether more augmented data can result in continued gains in model performance. To answer this, we experimented with {5, 10, 20} generated samples. For each number of generated samples, we also set the number of replaced tokens for the LM and the number of replaced non-terminals for CR to be {1, 3, 5}. We have described the distribution of non terminals in Table 1. All of these settings were tested against the 27,625 sentences from our validation set.

Phrase	S	M	L
NP	332	637	2562
VP	93	189	881
PP	54	130	690
ADJP	31	42	189
ADVP	16	27	126
FRAG	2	2	4

Table 1: Distribution of the number of phrases in the training data.

4.4 Results

Table 2 described the highest F1 scores for each augmentation strategy. The best F1 scores were taken for each strategy, across multiple hyperparameters. We found that synonym replacement still outperforms other augmentation strategies in small and medium dataset sizes.

Experiment	S	M	L
NoA	46.3 ± 0.5	61.4 ± 0.1	70.7 ± 0.1
SR	$\mathbf{53.0 \pm 0.2}$	$\mathbf{65.7 \pm 0.1}$	71.0 ± 0.0
MR	51.9 ± 0.2	61.7 ± 0.1	70.2 ± 0.0
LM	52.9 ± 0.1	63.3 ± 0.1	$\mathbf{73.3 \pm 0.2}$
CR-ADJP	47.8 ± 0.2	61.0 ± 0.1	71.2 ± 0.1
CR-ADVP	50.5 ± 0.3	61.9 ± 0.1	71.3 ± 0.1
CR-NP	52.1 ± 0.3	60.6 ± 0.1	70.2 ± 0.1
CR-PP	52.1 ± 0.1	62.4 ± 0.1	71.9 ± 0.1
CR-VP	52.9 ± 0.2	62.8 ± 0.1	72.8 ± 0.1

Table 2: Results for data augmentation experiments across different data set sizes. Top results for each data partition are marked in **bold**.

All augmentation methods tested seem to improve performance in terms of F1 for the small training set (50 sentences). When we look at the medium dataset, however, some methods such as CR-ADJP or CR-NP, start to have a negative impact compared to no augmentation settings. Even more augmentation strategies begin to show diminishing or negative effects on performance for the larger dataset (e.g., MR and CR-NP). This suggests that some of the augmented data might be detrimental for the model fine-tuning process.

To understand how the augmented data may start to hurt the original model's performance, we consider one original sentence processed using CR-NP strategy. For example, "Dr. Foutchner will arrange for an outpatient Holter monitor". In the case of the CR strategy, the augmentation algorithm draws an NP from another training sentence, resulting in "Dr. Foutchner will arrange for a T2 signal change" or "Dr. Foutchner will arrange for 10 beats". These augmented sentences are grammatical, but they lack cohesion. This phenomenon may impact the model negatively. Future work should explore strategies to control for this drift. For instance, by fine-tuning a large-scale language model to perform masked language modeling on sentences where a portion of tokens are provided in terms of phrasal category (XP) or functional category (part of speech tag), we might hybridize syntax-driven transformations and instantiate syntactic templates using large-scale language models.

We observed that among CR strategies, CR-NP performance seems to be worse compared to CR-VP or CR-PP, despite NP has the most occurrences in the training data. We suspect that the effectiveness of this strategy will heavily depend on the

	S			M			L		
	5	10	20	5	10	20	5	10	20
LM	50.6	51.5	50.6	61.2	60.8	61.0	71.1	70.8	70.6
CR-VP	50.5	52.0	52.3	61.9	62.3	62.5	71.9	72.3	72.3

Table 3: Comparison between CR-VP and LM augmentation. CR-VP holds more consistent performance across the number of generated sentences, while LM performance drops when the number of generated sentences is low.

scope of the constituency tag. NPs are usually located low in the constituency tree, while VPs are usually located toward the top.

The augmentation strategies explored in this work can be further divided into two groups: strategies that produce new vocabularies and strategies that do not produce new vocabularies. SR and LM methods fall into augmentation that produce new vocabularies. SR uses the Penn Treebank (Marcus et al., 1993) to generate synonyms of replaced tokens. LM use its word embedding to guess the masked target token and may generate new words that do not exist in the training data. The other strategies (MR and CR) rely solely on the current training dataset. This phenomenon suggests augmentation strategies that produce new vocabularies seem to be more effective. This is plausible since new words will make the fine-tuned model more robust to unseen data. Although CR does not generate new words like the LM and SR methods, it still performs competitively in comparison. The delta between F1 scores produced by CR-VP and LM with our best hyperparameters for all dataset sizes are remarkably small at around 0 0.5 points. The effect of simpler data augmentation strategies, SR and MR, seems to be diminishing as the data size increases; however, it is not the case with the LM and CR-VP strategies. They seem to perform well when more training data is available.

Looking at Table 3, the CR-VP augmentation strategy seems to show more consistent performance growth compared to the LM strategy. Whether it is 5, 10 or 20 sentences generated, CR-VP consistently trends upward as the number of augmented sentences increases (cf the instability of the LM). The average performance of the CR strategy shows an increased F1 as the number of synthetic sentences grows. In contrast, the average performance of the LM strategy is inconsistent and trending downward as the number of synthetic sentences increases.

Lastly, the performance of the CR strategy will also be affected by the performance of constituency parser component itself. For one of our augmented examples, the original sentence "She [$_{\text{VP}}$ had a workup by her neurologist] and an MRI [$_{\text{VP}}$ call with any fevers , chills , increasing weakness...]" was mutated into "She [$_{\text{VP}}$ had a workup by her neurologist] and an MRI [$_{\text{VP}}$ flare]". Here, the word *flare* was falsely predicted as a verb and thus erroneously predicted as a VP constituent, while the word *flare* here should be a part of *COPD flare* and classified as noun.

5 Conclusion and Future Work

In this work, we examined data augmentation with a large-scale language model (LM) and constituency tree mutation (ST). We compared these augmentation methods with a baseline and previously proposed strategies for data augmentation: synonym replacement (SR) and mention replacement (MR). We found that SR performance is still most effective, by a small margin, but the performance degrades quickly as the data size increased. We have also observed that both LM and CR retained their performance throughout larger dataset sizes. We also showed that CR performance seems to be consistent in its improvement as the augmented dataset size increases, while the LM showed degrading performance with more augmented data.

Future work should include improvements that hybridize the syntactic transformations with a large-scale language model. One possibility to increase the performance of the baseline language model is to train it to recognize phrase-level constituents and functional categories to understand more about constituency tags by first randomly swapping a few tokens with part of speech tags. For example, the original sentence is "I take my medicine.", then the pre-training sentence is "I VB my medicine." and "I take my NN.". We hypothesize that this pre-training will improve the prediction performance of the baseline language model that we used for CR augmentation by attending to functional categories. Another possibility is to assign different weights to datapoints that inform the model how much to "trust" augmented data compared to gold data. This weight could be in the form of different learning rate.

References

Jiangang Bai, Yujing Wang, Yiren Chen, Yaming Yang, Jing Bai, Jing Yu, and Yunhai Tong. 2021. Syntax-BERT: Improving pre-trained transformers with syntax trees. In *Proceedings of the 16th Conference of the European Chapter of the Association for Computational Linguistics: Main Volume*, pages 3011–3020, Online. Association for Computational Linguistics.

Xiang Dai and Heike Adel. 2021. An analysis of simple data augmentation for named entity recognition. pages 3861–3867.

Jacob Devlin, Ming-Wei Chang, Kenton Lee, and Kristina Toutanova. 2019. BERT: Pre-training of deep bidirectional transformers for language understanding. In *Proceedings of the 2019 Conference of the North American Chapter of the Association for Computational Linguistics: Human Language Technologies, Volume 1 (Long and Short Papers)*, pages 4171–4186, Minneapolis, Minnesota. Association for Computational Linguistics.

Bosheng Ding, Linlin Liu, Lidong Bing, Canasai Kruengkrai, Thien Hai Nguyen, Shafiq Joty, Luo Si, and Chunyan Miao. 2020. DAGA: Data augmentation with a generation approach for low-resource tagging tasks. In *Proceedings of the 2020 Conference on Empirical Methods in Natural Language Processing (EMNLP)*, pages 6045–6057, Online. Association for Computational Linguistics.

Steven Y. Feng, Varun Gangal, Jason Wei, Sarath Chandar, Soroush Vosoughi, Teruko Mitamura, and Eduard Hovy. 2021. A survey of data augmentation approaches for NLP. In *Findings of the Association for Computational Linguistics: ACL-IJCNLP 2021*, pages 968–988, Online. Association for Computational Linguistics.

John Hewitt and Christopher D. Manning. 2019. A structural probe for finding syntax in word representations. In *Proceedings of the 2019 Conference of the North American Chapter of the Association for Computational Linguistics: Human Language Technologies, Volume 1 (Long and Short Papers)*, pages 4129–4138, Minneapolis, Minnesota. Association for Computational Linguistics.

Sosuke Kobayashi. 2018. Contextual augmentation: Data augmentation by words with paradigmatic relations. In *Proceedings of the 2018 Conference of the North American Chapter of the Association for Computational Linguistics: Human Language Technologies, Volume 2 (Short Papers)*, pages 452–457, New Orleans, Louisiana. Association for Computational Linguistics.

Mitchell P. Marcus, Beatrice Santorini, and Mary Ann Marcinkiewicz. 1993. Building a large annotated corpus of English: The Penn Treebank. *Computational Linguistics*, 19(2):313–330.

George A. Miller. 1992. WordNet: A lexical database for English. In *Speech and Natural Language: Proceedings of a Workshop Held at Harriman, New York, February 23-26, 1992*.

Peng Qi, Yuhao Zhang, Yuhui Zhang, Jason Bolton, and Christopher D. Manning. 2020. Stanza: A python natural language processing toolkit for many human languages. *CoRR*, abs/2003.07082.

Husam Quteineh, Spyridon Samothrakis, and Richard Sutcliffe. 2020. Textual data augmentation for efficient active learning on tiny datasets. In *Proceedings of the 2020 Conference on Empirical Methods in Natural Language Processing (EMNLP)*, pages 7400–7410, Online. Association for Computational Linguistics.

Wilson L. Taylor. 1953. "cloze procedure": A new tool for measuring readability. *Journalism Quarterly*, 30(4):415–433.

Özlem Uzuner, Brett R. South, Shuying Shen, and Scott L Duvall. 2011. 2010 i2b2/va challenge on concepts, assertions, and relations in clinical text. *Journal of the American Medical Informatics Association : JAMIA*, 18 5:552–6.

Jason Wei, Dan Garrette, Tal Linzen, and Ellie Pavlick. 2021. Frequency effects on syntactic rule learning in transformers. In *Proceedings of the 2021 Conference on Empirical Methods in Natural Language Processing*, pages 932–948, Online and Punta Cana, Dominican Republic. Association for Computational Linguistics.

Jason Wei and Kai Zou. 2019. EDA: Easy data augmentation techniques for boosting performance on text classification tasks. In *Proceedings of the 2019 Conference on Empirical Methods in Natural Language Processing and the 9th International Joint Conference on Natural Language Processing (EMNLP-IJCNLP)*, pages 6382–6388, Hong Kong, China. Association for Computational Linguistics.

Le Zhang, Zichao Yang, and Diyi Yang. 2022. TreeMix: Compositional constituency-based data augmentation for natural language understanding. In *Proceedings of the 2022 Conference of the North American Chapter of the Association for Computational Linguistics: Human Language Technologies*, pages 5243–5258, Seattle, United States. Association for Computational Linguistics.

Query Processing and Optimization for a Custom Retrieval Language

Yakov Kuzin, Anna Smirnova, Evgeniy Slobodkin, and **George Chernishev**
Saint Petersburg University, Saint Petersburg, Russia
{yakov.s.kuzin, anna.en.smirnova, eugene.slobodkin, chernishev}@gmail.com

Abstract

Data annotation has been a pressing issue ever since the rise of machine learning and associated areas. It is well-known that obtaining high-quality annotated data incurs high costs, be they financial or time-related. In our previous work, we have proposed a custom, SQL-like retrieval language used to query collections of short documents, such as chat transcripts or tweets. Its main purpose is enabling a human annotator to select "situations" from such collections, i.e. subsets of documents that are related both thematically and temporally. This language, named Matcher, was prototyped in our custom annotation tool. Entering the next stage of development of the tool, we have tested the prototype implementation. Given the language's rich semantics, many possible execution options with various costs arise. We have found out we could provide tangible improvement in terms of speed and memory consumption by carefully selecting the execution strategy in each particular case. In this work, we present the improved algorithms and proposed optimization methods, as well as a benchmark suite whose results show the significance of the presented techniques. While this is an initial work and not a full-fledged optimization framework, it nevertheless yields good results, providing up to tenfold improvement.

1 Introduction

In recent years, rule-based approaches to various tasks pertaining to information extraction (IE) and natural language processing (NLP) have been "benched" by the academic community. Even ten years ago, rule-based systems were on their downfall of popularity (Chiticariu et al., 2013), and the situation does not seem to have changed now with the rise of machine learning models that are easily fine-tuned for any tasks and frameworks that provide even non-experienced users with all the necessary tools. Even the task of data annotation, which has been traditionally dealt with via manual labour, can now be simplified by annotation tools that leverage machine learning capabilities[1]. Methods such as few-shot or zero-shot learning can help deal with the problem of limited available data, and produce outstanding results in domain-independent natural language tasks.

However, rule-based approaches have held their ground in a specific area: industrial applications, especially those that require domain adaptation (Chiticariu et al., 2010b), such as biomedical information extraction (Kreimeyer et al., 2017). In settings that require high accuracy, the convenience of using an ML model can be traded off to obtain better results. However, using a *declarative* approach instead of a classical approach to IE (programs written in general-purpose programming languages intended for extraction of "hard-coded" features) adds the convenience and flexibility back. Additionally, using such approaches can help overcome issues with machine learning bias (Yapo and Weiss, 2018), unfortunate examples of which have been recorded many times.

Furthermore, the questions of performance and costs constitute a pressing issue. Using machine learning in an enterprise environment usually requires the company to both obtain expensive computational resources such as specialized GPUs and develop new ETL pipelines, given the need to protect the data that their customers provide. Furthermore, using an ML model might just not be fast or scalable enough for a business need. However, a rule-based approach to information extraction is scalable by definition, with the help of optimization and other techniques. Our project, Chat Corpora Annotator, implements a rule-based approach. It is intended for the task of data exploration and subsequent annotation. At present, its main use is exploring very long chat transcripts with extracting and annotating subsets of messages with open-domain tagsets defined by the user. A sim-

[1]A prominent example of this is prodi.gy by spaCy.

Proceedings of the 29th International Conference on Computational Linguistic, pages 61–70
October 12–17, 2022.

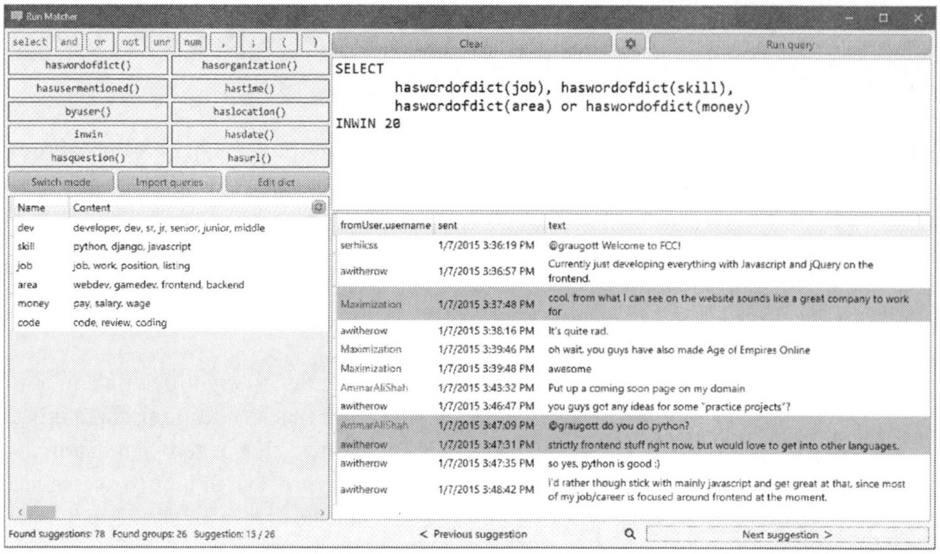

Figure 1: The Matcher interface implemented inside Chat Corpora Annotator. The left side of the window contains all of the available operators, as well as the word lists used for matching. The top frame contains a Matcher query, and the bottom frame contains its results, which can be navigated using the buttons below. The messages that match the query are highlighted in red. The query can be interpreted as extraction of mentions of job postings.

ple example of such extraction would be finding all subsets of messages in which the users of a chatroom make plans to meet in real life. Our previous paper presents the first version of the tool together with a detailed description of its intended usage (Smirnova et al., 2021). The semi-automatic rule-based extraction is implemented by our custom query language Matcher. It is a declarative, SQL-like language whose main purpose is to match over groups of messages according to the specified predicates and constraints. The supported predicates are all natural-language related, which makes the queries and their results easily interpretable. Additionally, Matcher supports complex Boolean querying and subqueries, which provide rich data exploration capabilities. Further on, we will provide the description of all supported operators and showcase several query examples on real data. Figure 1 presents the interface used to run Matcher queries.

The first version of Matcher was more of a prototype than an actual ready-to-use instrument, and, subsequently, the methods that actually retrieved and matched messages were implemented without optimization at all. Developing the second version, we ran into many performance-related issues while testing Matcher on large datasets, especially complex queries with several sub-queries, such as extremely long processing times. Therefore, we have proceeded with the decision to develop and study various query evaluation strategies for our language. Query optimization is an essential part of database query processing, so we reuse some of its core ideas in our approach. Overall, the contributions of this paper are:

1. A description of the next version of Matcher, which was extended by adding a new keyword.
2. A discussion of five query evaluation strategies which were implemented and benchmarked in the next version of CCA.
3. A benchmark suite which will provide repeatability of our experiments and may serve a basis for further studies concerning optimization of such queries.

The rest of this paper is organized as follows: Section 2 contains an overview of related work, Section 3 provides a description of our query language, Section 4 describes the algorithms that we propose for query optimization, and Section 5 and Section 6 describe the benchmark and showcase the experimental results. Finally, we give some concluding remarks in Section 7.

2 Related Work

2.1 Rule-Based Systems

Probably one of the most prominent examples, IBM's SystemT (Li et al., 2011), is an information extraction system that implements AQL — a declarative rule language that is intended for extracting structured information from unstructured documents. It is similar to SQL in syntax, and its output is presented as an SQL `view`. Below we will briefly discuss its query optimization approach. An interesting development worthy of mentioning is the rule-based NERL language (Chiticariu et al., 2010b) built on top of SystemT and intended for customized named entity recognition.

A different declarative approach is implemented in the DeepDive system (Zhang et al., 2017; Shin et al., 2015). They employ a language based on SQL and Datalog in order to facilitate the development of declarative programs for information extraction and subsequent use of this information, such as constructing knowledge bases.

Odinson (Valenzuela-Escárcega et al., 2020) is one of newest rule-based information extraction frameworks, presented in 2020. It features a system for annotating and essentially constructing a custom knowledge base, and a declarative pattern query language which is used for extracting information out of them. The language has the capabilities to run over not only tokens and token features, but graph-like annotations as well (such as syntactic dependencies). Internally, Odinson is based on a custom Lucene index, specifically implemented to index as much information about annotated documents as possible. This provides a large share of runtime optimization. Additionally, since not everything can be indexed, Odinson also contains a query compiler that optimizes the queries that involve syntax annotations, compiling them into a graph traversal pattern. The authors state that due to their optimizations, Odinson is 150,000 times faster than its predecessor Odin.

GATE (Cunningham et al., 2002) is a well-known IE system/framework which was first released in 2002. It features a possibility to construct annotators with JAPE (Java Annotation Patterns Engine), which is an imperative rule-based language adhering to the CSPL (Common Pattern Specification Language) standard. As far as we know, approaches based on CSPL cannot be optimized, as they produce a finite state transducer and have a set rule execution order.

Finally, another notable information extraction system is the UIMA Ruta framework (Klügl et al., 2016). It features an expressive matching language that allows building concise representations of matching rules. It is not declarative, similarly to GATE. However, the authors state that their language does not suffer from the drawbacks of CSPL, as it supports variable execution order, but they do not touch on optimization.

2.2 Query Optimization

Overall, query optimization is a well-developed and well-studied area. Starting out in 1979 with System R's optimizer (Selinger et al., 1979), studies of optimization allowed optimizers to become a standard and indispensable feature in all industrial DBMSes (Özsu and Valduriez, 2011). Some of the most prominent works of this area concern the Starburst and the Volcano optimizers. Overall, over the years optimization has accumulated a rich set of concepts and principles such as selectivity, interesting orders, minimization of intermediate results, data sketches (histograms) and many more.

However, query optimization for lesser-known purposes, such as query languages intended for information extraction, has not been properly explored. Further on, we will try to provide an overview of existing solutions. In their 2013 article (Chiticariu et al., 2010a), the authors of SystemT present an algebraic query optimizer for AQL. Unlike its main competitors, CSPL-based languages that use cascading grammars, AQL does not place evaluation order restrictions on its operators. This opens up the fundamental possibility of constructing an operator graph, and furthermore, many operator graphs for a single query, which in turn makes it possible to select the best one. The authors formally prove that the CSPL grammars cannot produce a finite state transducer that is faster than any algebraic graph, and compare the performance of SystemT and GATE on a rule-based Named Entity Recognition task. Their system won in both throughput and required memory.

The SQoUT project (Jain et al., 2009a) was a system that allowed its user to run structured queries over relation tuples extracted from natural language texts. The authors have implemented a full-fledged cost-based query optimizer for SQL over a database that stores such relation tuples. In their later article(Jain et al., 2009b), they consider join optimization for their system, focusing not only on performance, but on output quality, because in such a task it is critical: i.e., the relation tuples cannot be invalid. Their optimizer chooses between three join algorithms: Independent Join, Outer/Inner Join, and Zig-Zag Join. The authors provide a thorough evaluation of both performance and quality of output, and come to the conclusion that their optimizer is effective.

Finally, in their 2012 article, El-Helw et al. (El-Helw et al., 2012) introduce the concept of *extraction views*: database views whose data is obtained by running information extractors on specific document collections. The authors state that any extractor such as GATE or UIMA can be used for this purpose. They introduce a system that integrates SQL with such extractors, which can be used to build special tables out of tuples extracted from unstructured documents. Additionally, they provide a cost-based optimizer for SQL queries over such tables, which supports visualization of the used execution plan.

To the best of our knowledge, these are the only papers that concern optimizing queries for information extraction systems. However, none of them were intended for the task that we have formulated: extracting subsets of messages out of short text datasets, such as raw dumps of chats and tweets. They could not be adapted for the task either, as they are focused strictly on extracting pre-specified information, such as, for example, detecting phone numbers in a set of email documents. Whereas our approach is more oriented towards *discovery* of information that may match a specific, but rather loose pattern. This is prompted by the nature of chats and tweets, as they are often entangled and noisy, and traditional IE tools may fall short in the task we propose. At the same time, considering their optimization, such IE systems are necessary for both academic and industrial community and ensuring their performance is of priority. Therefore, reusing query optimization techniques from the database domain looks like a promising approach.

3 Matcher Query Language

Matcher query language consists of a basic set of rule-based matching operators, which can be combined into a *matcher* with Boolean operators, and which, in turn, can be combined into *matching groups* with commas. Furthermore, Matcher also contains a restriction operator `INWIN` and the `UNR` modifier, which will be explained below. The formal query syntax of Matcher is as follows:

```
query = SELECT body window
body = query_seq | restriction_seq
window = | INWIN N

query_seq =
  (query)
  | (query) ; query_seq

restriction_seq =
  restriction_seq_body
  | restriction_seq_body UNR

restriction_seq_body =
  restriction
  | restriction, restriction_seq

restriction =
  restriction AND restriction
  | restriction OR restriction
  | (restriction)
  | NOT restriction
  | condition
```

Here, bold denotes language keywords and regular denotes nonterminal symbols. Let us consider the language in a bottom-up fashion.

Formally, a *matcher* is a template that is matched against a single message in chat history. It consists of a Boolean expression which is evaluated for each message, and if it equals True, then the message is added to the output. Therefore, a *matching group* is a set of *matchers*, each of which provides a single message for the output. In the formal syntax, a *matcher* is described by the `restriction` nonterminal symbol, an individual rule-based matching operator by `condition`, and a *matching group* by the `restriction_seq`.

The currently the available set of rule-based matching operators is the following:

- `haswordofdict(dict)` matches messages that contain any word from a prespecified named list;
- `hasdate()`, `hastime()`, `haslocation()`, `hasorganization()`, `hasurl()` match messages that contain tokens with the respective Named Entity annotations[2];
- `hasusermentioned(user)` matches messages that contain a username mention in the text field;
- `byuser(user)` matches messages that contain a specified username in the user field;
- `hasquestion()` matches messages that contain at least one question-like sentence.

[2]Our system obtains NER annotations via external integration with a running CoreNLP instance.

Matcher relies on a simple data schema consisting of three fields: a username-like field, a date-like field, and a text-like field. CCA focuses on chat datasets, and we believe that this is a minimal restriction on such data.

Next, the body nonterminal symbol specifies two admissible types of queries: *matcher*-only and subquery-only. The first one consists only of *matchers* separated by commas. The second one requires nested `SELECT`s (separated by semicolons) inside the parent `SELECT`.

Matcher-only queries are intended for simple use-cases, while queries with subqueries provide flexibility by allowing to express complex patterns, constructing them in a bottom-up fashion. Such queries concatenate results of individual subqueries while checking additional restrictions such as distance between them and ordering. Matcher supports subqueries of arbitrary depth. Use-case examples are provided in Section 5.

The `window` nonterminal describes an optional `INWIN` clause. It provides a way to explicitly restrict the length of the window in which all matched messages should fit. For example, query `SELECT hasdate(), haswordofdict(meeting) INWIN 20` means that in each returned set of messages, the two messages that conform to the *matchers* must not be further away than 20 messages from each other. If not specified, this length is implicitly restricted to 50 on the language implementation level for performance reasons.

The current version of Matcher has been extended with a special `UNR` clause, which significantly improves the expressiveness of the language. It is a modifier that removes the match order constraint on *matching groups*. Without this clause, the outputs of each *matching group* are ordered according to their order in the query.

4 Query Processing

4.1 Basics

The goal of our query processor is to construct a list of answers, each answer being a list of integer message ids. Thus, all operations are performed on integer lists (groups) or lists of integer lists (group lists).

Due to the space constraints we will not present the pseudocode of algorithms, but we will sketch out the ideas behind them instead.

In general, Matcher's query evaluation consists of four phases, which correspond to functions in the source code:

1. **VisitQuery**. It is the first function that handles a submitted query. If there are subqueries in it, it obtains their results and then performs merging, calling **MergeQueries** which checks order and `INWIN` requirements. If there are no subqueries, i.e. the query contains only a *matching group*, then **VisitRestrictions** is called. After this, the output of **VisitQuery** is constructed by eliminating duplicates and sorting final message lists by their first message position. Note that **VisitQuery** is a recursive function that is run for each subquery.

2. **VisitRestrictions**. It obtains a group list in which the i-th group contains all messages that conform to the i-th *matcher* (the entire Boolean formula) and sorts it if necessary. This phase also handles the `UNR` clause by generating all possible permutations of the groups. This method calls **VisitCondition** to obtain message ids that conform to individual conditions.

3. **VisitCondition**. It queries the transcript to extract all messages that conform to a single predicate (`haswordofdict`, `byuser`, `hasdate`, `hastime`, etc).

4. **MergeRestrictions**. This function accepts a group list, where each list corresponds to an individual restriction. Items of these lists are message ids that conform to the respective Boolean formula. The output is another group list, but each group corresponds to an answer. Thus, **MergeRestrictions** constructs this list by taking ids from different input groups while checking the `INWIN` clause.

Our initial experiments demonstrated that there are two most expensive functions which needed to be optimized — **VisitCondition** and **MergeRestrictions** (see Fig. 4). The first one works by issuing calls to Lucene, which stores indexed chat transcript data. There are many possible straightforward methods, e.g. implementing reuse or setting up caching, tuning Lucene, using another storage layer and so on. In terms of DBMS query processing and optimization, this part is similar to the access method selection problem. On the other hand, optimizing **MergeRestrictions** resembles join optimization and it is trickier than **VisitCondition**.

For this paper, we have decided to develop several different strategies for optimizing this part. Let us consider in detail how a Matcher query is evaluated.

Query evaluation starts with the body of the main SELECT clause. Any SELECT can consist of either a sequence of nested subqueries or a sequence of *matchers*, i.e. a matching group.

If the body consists of n *matchers*, we find the ids of messages that satisfy the respective conditions, obtaining n groups of messages. Let us denote this stage with an asterisk (*). If the `UNR` modifier is used, all possible permutations of the obtained groups are generated, and if not, a single order (which is specified in the query) is considered. For each group order (that is, for each permutation), we merge the groups taking into account order constraints and the `INWIN` condition, i.e., we create lists of n ids, each element of which is an element of some group. We check the uniqueness of these lists, deleting those that are already in the resulting list, and add the rest to the output of the current query or subquery.

However, if the body consists of k subqueries, we process each subquery and merge the obtained lists, taking into account order constraints and the `INWIN` condition, obtaining a group list sequence. Merging produces lists that contain k groups, each of which is an element of the resulting list of the corresponding subquery. Thus, this is recursion — we process sequences of subqueries until we reach a subquery that does not have its own subqueries.

Now, for the **MergeRestrictions** phase we propose several different algorithms, namely:

1. N+NS: naive, no sort;
2. N+S: naive, with sort;
3. P+NS: position-based, no sort;
4. P+S: position-based, with sort;
5. H+S: histograms, with sort.

The first part of their name encodes method and shows whether the groups to be merged have been sorted at the (*) stage (i.e., when they were obtained).

4.2 N+NS: naive, no sort

The N+NS algorithm is the most basic version of all considered algorithms. It is a recursive algorithm which at first selects the first group and starts iterating over its values, launching itself for each individual value. This value will be the beginning of an answer, which is a list. Each launched instance has this partial answer as the first parameter and the remaining groups as the second. On subsequent recursion steps, the algorithm tries to add the next message id (taking it from the first group, out the remaining ones) to the partial answer. For this, it is necessary to check: 1) whether the id of previous message is smaller than the id of the current one, and 2) whether the `INWIN` restriction holds. If there are no suitable message ids in the considered list, then this recursion branch terminates. Thus, at each recursion step, the partial answer grows by a single id until all groups are checked.

4.3 N+S: naive, with sort

The N+S algorithm is the same, except that it leverages the fact that the contents of lists to merge are sorted. Thus, it makes possible to greatly reduce the number of recursive paths to traverse.

There is a number of differences from the N+NS algorithm. Firstly, it sorts each obtained group at the (*) stage in ascending order. Next, on the second and all subsequent recursive steps it conducts different checks to test whether the considered id can participate in the result.

More specifically, if the current message id goes beyond the `INWIN` restriction, further processing of the next elements of the current group stops. Indeed, due to the ascending order of the groups, all subsequent messages of this group definitely cannot fit into the window.

Such approach allows to early terminate the evaluation, which will have a good effect on the overall performance. However, sorting will incur additional costs, which should be taken into account and which we will experimentally evaluate.

4.4 P+NS: position-based, no sort

The next algorithm is built around the following idea: we should start merging groups from the smallest ones (in terms of their size) and finish with the largest one. Using this approach, we can reduce the number of recursive branches which do not satisfy the `INWIN` and order requirements. At the same time, the need of a novel approach to checking order requirements arises. The idea is illustrated in Figure 2. When we add an id to the resulting list we have to check that the id of previous message is smaller and that id of the next message

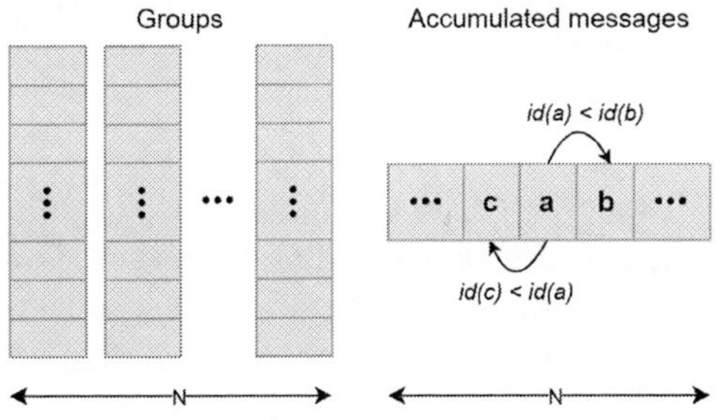

Figure 2: The P+NS algorithm

is greater (if they have been already placed). We call this class of algorithms position-based.

4.5 P+S: position-based, with sort

Similarly to P+NS, this algorithm exploits the idea of merging smallest groups first. But at the same time it relies on the sorting idea of the N+S algorithm. Thus, the P+S algorithm sorts each resulting group at the (*) stage, and at the start the algorithm is supplied with the number of messages in each group.

Then, similarly to the N+S, it is possible to prune a large number of recursive branches that do not satisfy the order and `INWIN` restrictions.

4.6 H+S: histograms with sort

The next stage in the development is the H+S algorithm, which uses equi-width histograms (Ioannidis, 2003) of message distribution. The idea is the following: unlike all previous algorithms which merged all groups at-a-time we merge groups two at-a-time.

At the same time, we try to merge groups that will result in as few intermediate results as possible first. This resembles the idea of classic optimization of a join sequence in SQL query processing, where the size of intermediates is reduced too. In order to estimate the sizes, we employ equi-width histograms, which are constructed in advance.

The algorithm itself is as follows. At first, we sort groups by their sizes. Then we iterate over triples of groups and try to assess the benefit for performing local permutations on them if their sizes are close enough. In our experiments (see Section 6) it was shown that sorting groups by their sizes (position-based approaches) already results in formidable improvement, therefore we should build our next algorithm upon this idea.

Assessing benefits of permutations is done in the following way. Suppose that we have groups A, B, C which we have to merge, and they are of similar size. We consider the following three permutations: ((AB)C), ((BC)A), and ((AC)B) which represent different evaluation orders. Each of them is assessed by "intersecting" histograms of the central part. After the intersection, we estimate the size of the intermediate result using obtained histograms. Then we select the evaluation order that corresponds to the smallest histogram.

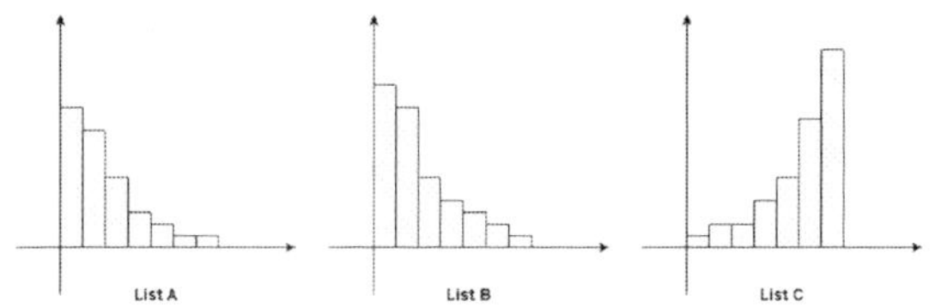

Figure 3: Distribution Example

Consider the example presented in Figure 3. Suppose that we have to merge A, B, and C lists with the message distributions as shown in the figure. It is evident that it is better to merge A and C (B and C) first than A and B. This way we will discard a lot of intermediates as soon as possible.

This approach will not provide performance improvement if there is an identical data distribution in all considered groups. But at the same time it will not incur a significant overhead except the histogram construction phase, which can be done in advance.

This is a prototype of a full-fledged optimizer intended to demonstrate its viability in our setting.

5 Benchmark

To ensure repeatability we have created a benchmark which consists of four queries and a message set. This message set contains the first 1 million messages from the freeCodeCamp Gitter Chat dataset, available on Kaggle[3]. Its Lucene index takes around 100MB of disk space.

Listing 1: Query 1 (Q1)

```
SELECT
  hasword(job), hasword(code),
  hasusermentioned(Kadams223)
UNR INWIN 40
```

The Q1 query matches a group of three messages that have words related to jobs, words related to code and a mention of a specific username. It can

[3]https://www.kaggle.com/datasets/freecodecamp/all-posts-public-main-chatroom

be interpreted as extracting a discussion that the specified user has been actively partaking in, receiving many replies. This is a simple query that illustrates the concept behind the UNR clause. The results of the *matchers* are not ordered in accordance to their order in the query, but the whole group should fit into a window of 40 messages. Note in that the following listings haswordofdict was shortened to hasword for better readability.

Listing 2: Query 2 (Q2)

```
SELECT
  hasword(job), hasword(skill),
  hasword(skill), hasword(area),
  hasword(money)
INWIN 40
```

Q2 extracts a group of five messages that discuss coding job listings with the mentions of the area of the job, required skill and the salary. This is a simple query with no subqueries, however, it has many *matchers* and a window length of 40 messages in which the extracted group should fit.

Listing 3: Query 3 (Q3)

```
SELECT
  (SELECT
    hasword(job), hasword(skill),
    hasword(code), byuser(Lumiras)
    INWIN 60
  );
  (SELECT
    byuser(Lumiras) AND hasword(issue)
  )
INWIN 200
```

The Q3 query extracts the following information: a discussion of job search and coding languages in which user Lumiras took part, and it is followed by an issue alert by the same user. This query contains two subqueries, the first of which has a medium-sized window, and the second one has a Boolean AND which specifies that the output of this *matching group*, containing a single message, must be by the specified user and contain a reference to an issue.

Listing 4: Query 4 (Q4)

```
SELECT
  (SELECT
    hasword(job), hasword(skill),
    hasword(code), byuser(Lumiras)
  );
  (SELECT
    hasword(job), hasword(skill),
    hasword(code), byuser(odrisck)
    INWIN 40
  );
  (SELECT
    hasword(job), hasword(skill),
    hasword(code), byuser(odrisck)
    INWIN 40
  )
INWIN 300
```

Q4 extracts three message groups, each of which discusses job search and coding languages. User Lumiras participates in the first group, and user odrisck takes part in the second and the third. This query contains three similar subqueries and a large window for the groups to fit in.

6 Experiments and Discussion

Experimental evaluation was conducted on a PC with the following characteristics: 8-core Intel®Core™ i7-11800H CPU @ 2.30GHz, 16 GB RAM, running Windows 10.0.19042.1645 (20H2/October2020Update).

The current version of CCA is implemented in C# (.NET 6, WPF) using the following libraries: Antlr4, Lucene.Net 4.8.0, Newtonsoft.Json, and SoftCircuits.CsvParser. To obtain accurate measurements, we have used BenchmarkDotNet v0.13.1[4]. It was run with default parameters, a confidence interval of 99.9% was calculated by the benchmark (as a different number of runs was used in each case), and we manually checked that relative error was less than 2%. Our source code is available publicly[5].

In our first experiment we have compared the four initial versions of the algorithm: N+NS, N+S, P+NS and P+S. For this, we used the first four queries of our benchmark. The overall results are presented in Table 1.

To provide better insights into the results, we have also constructed a stacked barchart presented in Figure 4. It shows four approaches each depicted by its own bar. Each bar is divided into parts that correspond to the contribution of each method.

Our experiments have clearly demonstrated that all of the proposed strategies are superior in performance to the basic N+NS. Overall, P+S is the most efficient approach, which noticeably beats N+S and N+NS, and to a lesser extent P+NS. It was possible to obtain more that 10x speedup for a subset of queries.

The next observation is that sorting of group elements is almost free in terms of time. Sorting is conducted inside the **VisitRestriction** function and

[4]https://github.com/dotnet/BenchmarkDotNet

[5]https://github.com/yakovypg/Chat-Corpora-Annotator

Query	Msgs	N+NS	Impr	N+S	Impr	P+NS	Impr	P+S	Impr
Q1	1M	2253.5	-	1232.8	1.8x	209.4	10.8x	**207.0**	10.9x
Q2	1M	4260.6	-	1954.6	2.2x	530.6	8.0x	**419.1**	10.2x
Q3	1M	4354.1	-	2248.0	1.9x	408.1	10.7x	**379.2**	11.5x
Q4	1M	11615.2	-	6193.5	1.9x	2016.7	5.8x	**1318.6**	8.8x
Total	—	22483.4	-	11628.9	1.9x	3164.8	7.1x	**2323.9**	9.7x

Table 1: Overall results

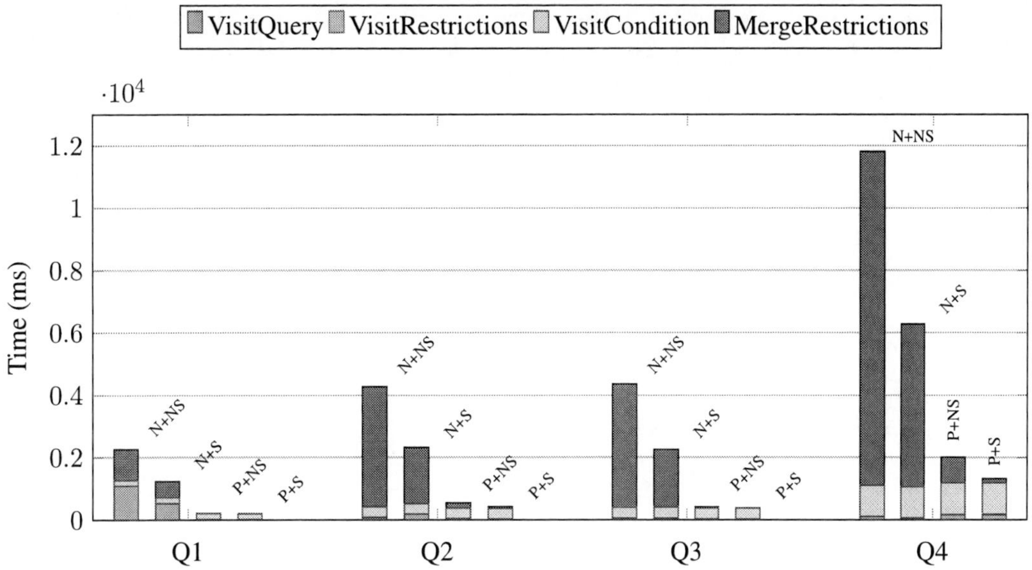

Figure 4: In-depth results

the figure shows that its presence has almost no impact on the bar height.

Listing 5: Query 5 (Q5)

```
SELECT
  byuser(sludge256),
  byuser(sludge256),
  byuser(trisell) OR byuser(seahik) OR
  byuser(odrisck) OR byuser(jsonify) OR
  byuser(cerissa) OR byuser(mykey007) OR
  byuser(AhsanBudhani) OR
  hasusermentioned(seahik)
INWIN 50
```

The second experiment concerned out last strategy, H+S. H+S does not always beat P+S, but it never loses to it, either. We have added the Q5 to our benchmark as an example on which H+S beats P+S: it takes 1479 ms compared to 1865 ms, thus providing 25% improvement.

7 Conclusion and Future Work

In this paper, we have presented and described our custom query language Matcher, intended for exploration and annotation of large natural language datasets such as chat transcripts. The main body of our work consisted in optimizing one of Matcher's execution stages that deals with merging the results of individual parts of the query, which in essence resembles join optimization. We have created five algorithms and a benchmark of five queries to test them against. We have not presented a proper optimizer, but a collection of simple techniques that nevertheless yield surprisingly good results, providing up to 10x improvement. All this warrants further investigation. Concerning our future work, the first evident direction is to implement a proper cost model, design rules for enumerating plan space, employ more sophisticated statistics and estimators of intermediate result sizes. Next, looking at graphs for the P+S algorithm, one may notice that for Q4, Lucene index access has become the most costly part and thus, it is necessary to address this. There are many approaches to optimizing Lucene index access which can be investigated. Finally, note that Matcher itself does not support variables so far, however, it is a necessary feature and it will have impact on optimization.

Acknowledgments

We would like to thank Kirill Smirnov for his comments on statistics for result processing.

References

Laura Chiticariu, Rajasekar Krishnamurthy, Yunyao Li, Sriram Raghavan, Frederick Reiss, and Shivakumar Vaithyanathan. 2010a. SystemT: An Algebraic Approach to Declarative Information Extraction. In *Proceedings of the 48th Annual Meeting of the Association for Computational Linguistics*, pages 128–137, Uppsala, Sweden. Association for Computational Linguistics.

Laura Chiticariu, Rajasekar Krishnamurthy, Yunyao Li, Frederick Reiss, and Shivakumar Vaithyanathan. 2010b. Domain Adaptation of Rule-Based Annotators for Named-Entity Recognition Tasks. In *Proceedings of the 2010 Conference on Empirical Methods in Natural Language Processing*, pages 1002–1012, Cambridge, MA. Association for Computational Linguistics.

Laura Chiticariu, Yunyao Li, and Frederick R. Reiss. 2013. Rule-Based Information Extraction is Dead! Long Live Rule-Based Information Extraction Systems! In *Proceedings of the 2013 Conference on Empirical Methods in Natural Language Processing*, pages 827–832, Seattle, Washington, USA. Association for Computational Linguistics.

Hamish Cunningham, Diana Maynard, Kalina Bontcheva, and Valentin Tablan. 2002. GATE: an Architecture for Development of Robust HLT applications. In *Proceedings of the 40th Annual Meeting of the Association for Computational Linguistics*, pages 168–175, Philadelphia, Pennsylvania, USA. Association for Computational Linguistics.

Amr El-Helw, Mina H. Farid, and Ihab F. Ilyas. 2012. Just-in-time information extraction using extraction views. In *Proceedings of the 2012 ACM SIGMOD International Conference on Management of Data*, SIGMOD '12, pages 613–616, New York, NY, USA. Association for Computing Machinery.

Yannis Ioannidis. 2003. The history of histograms (abridged). In *Proceedings of the 29th International Conference on Very Large Data Bases - Volume 29*, VLDB '03, page 19–30. VLDB Endowment.

Alpa Jain, Panagiotis Ipeirotis, and Luis Gravano. 2009a. Building query optimizers for information extraction: the SQoUT project. *ACM SIGMOD Record*, 37(4):28–34.

Alpa Jain, Panagiotis G. Ipeirotis, AnHai Doan, and Luis Gravano. 2009b. Join Optimization of Information Extraction Output: Quality Matters! In *2009 IEEE 25th International Conference on Data Engineering*, pages 186–197. ISSN: 2375-026X.

Peter Klügl, Martin Toepfer, Philip-Daniel Beck, Georg Fette, and Frank Puppe. 2016. UIMA Ruta: Rapid development of rule-based information extraction applications. *Natural Language Engineering*, 22(1):1–40.

Kory Kreimeyer, Matthew Foster, Abhishek Pandey, Nina Arya, Gwendolyn Halford, Sandra F Jones, Richard Forshee, Mark Walderhaug, and Taxiarchis Botsis. 2017. Natural language processing systems for capturing and standardizing unstructured clinical information: A systematic review. *Journal of Biomedical Informatics*, 73:14–29.

Yunyao Li, Frederick Reiss, and Laura Chiticariu. 2011. SystemT: A Declarative Information Extraction System. In *Proceedings of the ACL-HLT 2011 System Demonstrations*, pages 109–114, Portland, Oregon. Association for Computational Linguistics.

P. Griffiths Selinger, M. M. Astrahan, D. D. Chamberlin, R. A. Lorie, and T. G. Price. 1979. Access path selection in a relational database management system. In *Proceedings of the 1979 ACM SIGMOD international conference on Management of data*, SIGMOD '79, pages 23–34, New York, NY, USA. Association for Computing Machinery.

Jaeho Shin, Sen Wu, Feiran Wang, Christopher De Sa, Ce Zhang, and Christopher Ré. 2015. Incremental Knowledge Base Construction Using DeepDive. *Proceedings of the VLDB Endowment International Conference on Very Large Data Bases*, 8(11):1310–1321.

Anna Smirnova, Evgeniy Slobodkin, and George Chernishev. 2021. Situation-based multiparticipant chat summarization: a concept, an exploration-annotation tool and an example collection. In *Proceedings of the 59th Annual Meeting of the Association for Computational Linguistics and the 11th International Joint Conference on Natural Language Processing: Student Research Workshop*, pages 127–137, Online. Association for Computational Linguistics.

Marco A. Valenzuela-Escárcega, Gus Hahn-Powell, and Dane Bell. 2020. Odinson: A fast rule-based information extraction framework. In *Proceedings of the 12th Language Resources and Evaluation Conference*, pages 2183–2191, Marseille, France. European Language Resources Association.

Adrienne Yapo and Joseph W. Weiss. 2018. Ethical Implications of Bias in Machine Learning. In *HICSS*.

Ce Zhang, Christopher Ré, Michael Cafarella, Christopher De Sa, Alex Ratner, Jaeho Shin, Feiran Wang, and Sen Wu. 2017. DeepDive: declarative knowledge base construction. *Communications of the ACM*, 60(5):93–102.

M. Tamer Özsu and Patrick Valduriez. 2011. *Principles of Distributed Database Systems*, 3rd edition. Springer Publishing Company, Incorporated.

Rule Based Event Extraction for Artificial Social Intelligence

Remo Nitschke*, **Yuwei Wang***, **Chen Chen***, **Adarsh Pyarelal***, **Rebecca Sharp**†
*University of Arizona, Tucson, Arizona, USA
†Lex Machina, Tucson, Arizona, USA
{nitschke, wangyw, chencc33, adarsh}@arizona.edu

Abstract

Natural language (as opposed to structured communication modes such as Morse code) is by far the most common mode of communication between humans, and can thus provide significant insight into both individual mental states and interpersonal dynamics.

As part of DARPA's Artificial Social Intelligence for Successful Teams (ASIST) program, we are developing an AI agent team member that constructs and maintains models of their human teammates and provides appropriate task-relevant advice to improve team processes and mission performance. One of the key components of this agent is a module that uses a rule-based approach to extract task-relevant events from natural language utterances in real time, and publish them for consumption by downstream components.

In this case study, we evaluate the performance of our rule-based event extraction system on a recently conducted ASIST experiment consisting of a simulated urban search and rescue mission in Minecraft. We compare the performance of our approach with that of a zero-shot neural classifier, and find that our approach outperforms the classifier for all event types, even when the classifier is used in an oracle setting where it knows how many events should be extracted from each utterance.

1 Introduction

Humans communicate with each other using both explicit (e.g., written and spoken natural language) and implicit (e.g., tone of voice, body language) modalities. While we posit that an artificially intelligent (AI) agent needs to handle both of these modalities to serve as an effective teammate on a hybrid human-machine team, in this paper, we focus on the former.

To that end, here we present a case study describing our approach for extracting events relevant to team coordination (e.g., instructions, requests, knowledge-sharing statements about the locations of people and objects, etc.) in real-time from natural language dialog. This was carried out in the context of DARPA's Artificial Social Intelligence for Successful Teams (ASIST) program,[1] a 4.5 year program aimed at developing technologies for imbuing artificial agents with *social* intelligence, i.e., the ability to construct and maintain models of their human teammates in order to provide more effective assistance. The program is structured around five large-scale experiments. One of the primary goals of these experiments is to evaluate the AI agents developed in the program on their ability to successfully predict human behavior and improve team processes. In order to do this, the agents need to understand (and perhaps contribute to) the dialog that takes place between their teammates.

This case study focuses on the third of these five experiments (ASIST Study 3), in which teams consisting of three humans and an AI advisor must work together to rescue as many victims as possible within a limited time. The mission takes place in a collapsed office building simulated in Minecraft. The human players participate remotely, communicating with each other using voice chat.[2] The goal of our event extraction component is to detect specific team coordination-related events, and relay them to AI agents, who then update their understanding of the state of the team members and the mission. The event extraction component is embedded into a larger architecture, which is described in our preregistration document (Pyarelal, 2022, 5).

Critically, the actual *design* of these missions is subject to change with little notice. There is no training data for supervised approaches, and the specificity of the domain means that many open-domain approaches are unsuitable. For these rea-

[1] https://www.darpa.mil/program/artificial-social-intelligence-for-successful-teams

[2] For further details on the experimental design, see Huang et al. (2022a).

Proceedings of the 29th International Conference on Computational Linguistic, pages 71–84
October 12–17, 2022.

sons (described further in § 2) we employ a rule-based approach for our event extraction component. This allows us to rapidly pivot and adapt to changes in requirements, as well as encode details of the specific domain.

In this setting, this work provides these key contributions:

1. Case study comparison of a rule-based and a zero-shot approach to team coordination event extraction in a (semi) real-world scenario. We describe each approach and discuss the advantages and drawbacks of each. We also show that, at least in this setting with these constraints, the rule-based system outperforms the zero-shot system and is more flexible, with richer representations.

2. Evaluation dataset annotated for twenty communication events. This data can be used to evaluate other approaches to the same task, as well as serving as an example of what to do (and not do) when designing an annotation task for event extraction.[3]

2 Motivation for Rule-Based Approach

While most current academic research focuses on machine learning (ML) based approaches to information extraction (Ahmad et al., 2021; Du and Cardie, 2020a; Nguyen et al., 2016a; Tozzo et al., 2018; Chiticariu et al., 2013), here we use a rule-based approach that was developed in response to the specific constraints of the task and the ASIST program.

1. **Rapid adaptation.** The experimental setup of ASIST is subject to change at each experiment. Thus, this is a dynamic domain where entities, events, and relations are likely to change dramatically. Hence we need a system that can quickly and reliably adapt to such changes. Further, it would be near-impossible to annotate data and train or fine-tune a neural agent on the new vocabulary of a study *prior* to its actual execution. By using rules, we can simply add, modify, or remove rules as needed. In this way, adaption is straightforward and endlessly repeatable.

2. **Structured events.** In ASIST, communicative events that shed light on individual cognitive states and team processes are of particular interest for downstream components. These events generally have a complex structure with one or more arguments. Our rule-based system allows an unlimited number of arguments for events and allows events to become arguments of other events. This leads to highly nested, but still interpretable structures. While complex structures are certainly possible with ML approaches, they are not what is supported by zero-shot approaches and we simply do not have annotated datasets of the necessary size to train such a model.

3. **Transparency.** A rule-based approach allows our system's decisions to be immediately inspectable, which helps with maintainability. The transparency of rules also makes it easier for us to inject domain knowledge into the system.[4] ML based approaches can provide attention weights, but these are not necessarily an interpretation of why the system made the prediction it did (Jain and Wallace, 2019), and regardless, they are not straightforwardly actionable.

3 Related Work

Rule-based approaches to event extraction (EE) have a long tradition in previous work (e.g., Appelt and Onyshkevych, 1998; Cunningham et al., 2002; Levy and Andrew, 2006; Hunter et al., 2008; Valenzuela-Escárcega et al., 2018; Sharp et al., 2019). These rules were written over a variety of language forms, from surface to syntactic or semantic structures. Here we use rules that combine surface and syntactic forms (Valenzuela-Escárcega et al., 2015), to allow for richer representations while also mitigating the effect of parsing errors resulting from imperfect transcriptions from the automated speech recognition system.

That said, much of the recent literature is on machine learning approaches to EE (Nguyen et al., 2016b; Liu et al., 2018; Sha et al., 2018; Wadden et al., 2019; Du and Cardie, 2020b; Nguyen and Nguyen, 2019; Xiang and Wang, 2019, *inter alia*).

[3]Due to some issues we found with our annotations described in § 5.1, we will release our annotated data set in its original form and in its corrected version.

[4]For example, due to the nature of the mission, we know that when players interact with unnamed entities, those entities can only be victims. So a statement such as "*I will go get the guy in A3*", must be about saving a victim. We can easily bake this knowledge into our rules.

Much of this work, however, relies on supervision, a luxury we do not have in this setting.

With the rise of large pretrained neural models, there are now several approaches to common natural language processing tasks that do not train or fine-tune a model, but instead use *prompting* to glean desired information from the knowledge already contained in the model (e.g., Wei et al., 2021; Liu et al., 2021; Min et al., 2021). This category of approach is desirable in scenarios such as ours, where annotated data is unavailable and would be difficult to produce at scale. For this reason, we compare our rule-based approach to a zero-shot approach based on prompting. In § 7, we show that for our scenario, the rule-based approach performed better and was able to produce richer representations.

4 Approach

Our rule-based EE system uses the Odin (Valenzuela-Escárcega et al., 2016) event extraction framework, which consists of an expressive, declarative rule language and a runtime system for applying the rules. More specifically, we have an Odin rule grammar that extracts two broad types of events from natural language: (i) *simple events* that do not have arguments,[5] and (ii) *complex events*, that can take other events as arguments.

Each event is associated with a unique span of text and is assigned a label by the rule that extracts it. The event labels we are using are organized into a hierarchical ontology. If a rule assigns a label to an event from this ontology, the parents of that label in the ontology are also assigned as labels for that event.[6]

Our system currently contains 420 active rules. These map to a total of 238 event labels, including both parent labels as well as the labels for the events we intentionally target.[7] For example, if our system detects a event label for a specific room on the map (example: "A4"), it will output that specific event label and all its parent labels like so: "Concept > EventLike > Location > Infrastructure > Room > A4".[8] This allows us to look at outputs at any level of granularity and define event arguments at any level of granularity. That is, we can define an event that only requires an "A4" label as a possible argument, or else we can define an event that takes a "Location" event label as a possible argument.

Odin's support for nested patterns allows the user to implement recursive passes on the data, as well as specifying at which pass the system should match against which specific rules. For our purposes, we use this to first look for simple events only, and then on later passes we look for complex events. The passes are *recursive* because prior extractions are part of the input for later passes. For example, a "Room" event that was extracted in pass 3 can be an argument of a "Search" event in pass 6, which can in turn be an argument of an "Instruction" event in pass 12. Figure 1 shows a visual representation of a sample utterance and the events extracted from it.

The code, rules, and documentation for our approach are publicly available on our github repository.[9]

4.1 The Label Ontology and Nested Events

Our event labels we are using are organized in a hierarchical ontology. We present a sample of this ontology in the appendix, page 13. This allows us to access labels at different levels of granularity. For example, in this domain there are different subtypes of victim entities – thus, we have different rules and labels for each sub-type. All sub-types of the victim label are hierarchically organized within a general *Victim* label. When we write event rules that need to take a *Victim*-type label as an argument (for example, the *Save* event), we can simply specify the higher ranking general *Victim* label as a possible argument, which will automatically target all subordinated labels as well. If we need to specify an event that only targets a very specific kind of victim, then that is equally possible. The nested ontology allows us to generalize over events while still keeping as much granularity as we want.

Our system does not distinguish between entities and events; it treats every label as an event. Events take other events as arguments (if so specified), leading to nested event structures. This allows us to generate complex and informative label

[5]Simple events are mostly entities, but they can also be actions or events without arguments. For this reason we prefer to call them events, as opposed to entities.

[6]See § 4.1 for details.

[7]Due to the hierarchical nature of the ontology, some event labels are never exported by a rule directly, they exist only as parents for grouping. These parent event labels can still serve as arguments of other events.

[8]Note that we do not use the term *Event* in a strict way, locations are not events in a classic or true sense, but as in our implementation they can possibly have "arguments" (i.e., relative positions, etc.), we consider them *EventLike*.

[9]Please note that v4.1.5 is the version that used for this paper. This version can be found here: https://github.com/clulab/tomcat-text/tree/v4.1.5

structures. In Figure 1, there is a *DeliberatePlan* label that takes a *MoveTo* label as a topic argument. The *MoveTo* label itself takes a *Deictic* label as a target argument. In the exported JSON, the *DeliberatePlan* label will contain this entire hierarchical structure and all superordinate labels. We present a full JSON output for the above example in the appendix, page 12.

Neural event extraction often uses a named entity recognition (NER) model to find all entities that can serve as arguments for events. While we consider all labels as "events" for practical purposes, we do have classes of labels that fall under "entities" in the ontology. However, for the actual implementation, they operate the same way as "events" do in our system. Since our events can take other events as arguments (and are not limited to entities), we can generate more informative relationships between events, and are not limited to entities as possible arguments.

4.2 Rule Writing for Dynamic Domains

The experimental setup of ASIST changes with each new experiment. These changes can be small, such as new types of player interactions, or they can entail changing the entire base task that players perform itself. While we know ahead of time that changes will happen, we can never completely predict how players will communicate under the changed environment. This has lead us to adopt a 2-stage style of rule writing:

1. **Predictive Rule Writing**: In this stage we know what the domain will be, but we do not have any actual data yet. We write rules that aim to predict *how* players will talk about certain events.

2. **Subject Data Informed Rule Writing**: Once we receive pilot data, we evaluate our predictive rules on that data and make changes to them accordingly to prepare a improved, frozen version of our system that is deployed for the actual data collection.

This approach has helped us to manage rapid adaption, while retaining a high standard of results. For an example of one of our rules please refer to the Example Rule with Commentary in the appendix.

5 Data

In order to quantitatively evaluate our approach and highlight shortcomings, we annotated an evaluation dataset[10] of in-mission dialog transcriptions for several key team coordination-related events. The dynamic nature of the experiments in ASIST means that annotations for ASIST Study 3 cannot be used as training data for ASIST Study 4 and ASIST Study 5. For this reason we (a) only annotated enough for evaluating our approaches (rather than training), and (b) only annotated for key events, which were more likely to remain central, even as the experimental paradigm shifts.

Our annotated data is drawn from live mission dialog and constitutes a subset of the ASIST study 3 dataset (Huang et al., 2022b). The dialog is transcribed in real-time using the Google Cloud Speech automatic speech recognition (ASR) system. We do not manually correct the transcription errors, as we are interested in exploring what can be achieved by our EE system in a realistic, live scenario. Due to the nature of its origin, the utterances are often messy and grammatically incorrect. Further, they contain filler phrases, repetitions, and interruptions. For example:

> *okay okay yeah so many patients I need picked up was marker with the SOS*

As mentioned above, we chose a set of 20 event labels to evaluate (see appendix for detailed explanations), consisting of labels we considered most important or interesting to us in the context of the ASIST program, and thus more likely to stay relevant. Specifically, we selected:

- 'Superset' events that account for multiple types of events. For example, a "Plan" event subsumes different kinds of utterances that are indicative of planning activity (see appendix for details).

- Events highly specific to our use case, such as "RescueInteractions".[11]

- Events where we were unsure of the specific label's performance (recall that the primary purpose of the data is to evaluate the validity of our approach).

[10]The dataset is publicly available at `https://osf.io/6hr8t/`.

[11]This event type subsumes different actions that players can do with/to victims.

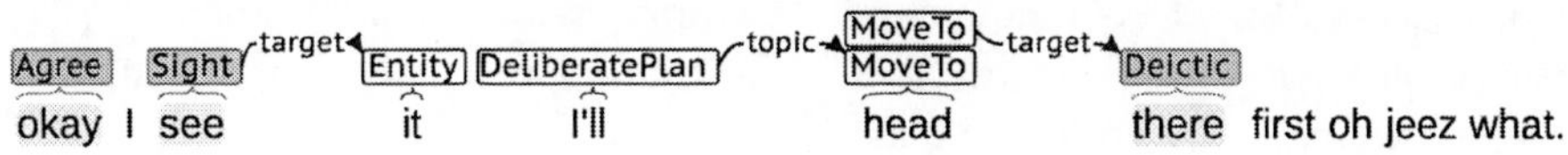

Figure 1: Visualization of extractions produced by our rule-based system. Note that some events are simple events without arguments, while others are complex, such as the "Agree" and " Sight" events respecitvely. Additionally, events can nest, as with the "DeliberatePlan" event, which takes the "MoveTo" event as an argument. Finally, note that the utterances that serve as input are often not grammatically well-formed.

Of our 20 labels, nine are simple events (entities) and eleven represent complex events.

We tasked annotators with annotating 3686 utterances of game dialog for the labels in our set. Specifically, we asked that for each event, they (a) mark the span of all arguments, and (b) label the event as a whole. We did not ask them to indicate the labels of arguments themselves.

Concurrently, we also annotated a subset of the same data internally for precision alone[12]. This precision-based evaluation was done to gain more fine-grained insight into the arguments selected by our event labels.

5.1 Annotation Issues and Lessons Learned

We provided a manual for our two annotators with descriptions of each event type and some typical examples of how they show up in the natural language utterances. In an initial 90-minute training session, we discussed each event and walked annotators through some examples. Subsequently, we let them annotate a test set which we used to calculate inter-annotator agreement (Cohen's kappa = 0.7451).

After annotations were complete, it was evident that our system performed significantly worse when evaluated against the annotated set than it had in internal evaluations conducted for ASIST Study 1 and ASIST Study 2. We quickly realized that the annotators had slightly different conceptualizations of our events than we thought or intended. As a result, they were essentially annotating for a different task than the one we originally planned.

This was caused by a few mistakes on our part. We underestimated the degree to which the annotators would need to be intimately familiar with the domain. Their relative unfamiliarity with the domain caused them to miss instances of events that they would otherwise have identified. Another issue we observed was that annotators only annotated certain action-related events if it could be inferred that the player actually performed that action. For example, compare the following utterances:

1. *I am going to A3*
2. *We should go to A3 next*

Annotators tended to give the first utterance a "Movement" label, but not the second. However, in the context of ASIST, we want to apply a "Movement" label to both, as we would like our AI agent to be able to better predict future actions, not simply identify current and past ones.

In order to address this issue, we manually corrected all instances of disagreement between our system and the annotators. After removing same-utterance duplicates, we had 3920 annotated labels. Of those, there were 2817 disagreements with our system.[13] After manual corrections, we found 1303 disagreements remaining.[14] We would like to remark that we did not make any changes of our codebase during this process.

This method of correction is not ideal, as it risks instilling bias. If only disagreements are examined, then we could incorrectly bake in false negatives that our system and the annotators both missed. The same is potentially true for false positives from both (though due to the general nature of the issues, this was less of a concern). To check on this clear risk for bias, we subsampled 20 instances of agreement between our annotators and our system for each of our 20 event labels[15] and checked those samples for any inaccuracies. We found that in our set of 20*20 decisions, only two were faulty (one "Precedence" and one "Instruction"). Finally, we also checked 50 utterances where neither annotators nor our system had assigned any event labels. We found that in 50 utterances, there were

[12]This involved running our system on the data and manually annotating the output and its argument structure as either correct or incorrect.

[13]These were either cases where our system assigned a label and the annotators did not, or the inverse case.

[14]This means that annotators were correct in their disagreement a little under 50% of the time.

[15]Two event labels had fewer than 20 instances of agreement: "Search" and "RescueInteractions".

again only two instances where both annotators and our system had missed a "CriticalVictim" label. No other issues were found. Given this, we use the corrected annotations to evaluate both the zero-shot baseline as well as the rule-based system. We found that the corrected annotations improved the performance of *both our system and the zero-shot baseline*.

As a takeaway, we recommend creating internal test annotations to compare against annotator work at the beginning of the annotation process. By doing a mix of qualitative comparison and calculating inter-annotator agreement between the internal annotations and annotator work, this kind of situation can be avoided.

6 Evaluation

We evaluate our rule-based approach at two different levels of granularity: coarse and fine-grained. For the former, we compare the performance of our approach to that of a zero-shot classifier (see § 6.1).

For the coarse-grained evaluation, we evaluated whether the correct labels were assigned to utterances, without checking for argument structure or spans. A given utterance may contain multiple events with the same label.[16] For simplicity in this evaluation, and to streamline comparison with the zero-shot approach, here we evaluate extractions on a presence-only basis. That is, if the annotator assigned one "Victim" label to an utterance, and our EE system assigned two "Victim" labels to the same utterance, we consider this correct for the purposes of evaluation.

For the fine-grained evaluation, we annotated a subset of our data for the precision of the argument structure of our outputs. We only consider outputs that we had already annotated as correct. If all their arguments match for the correct event, we consider the extraction as a true positive.[17]

During our evaluation process, we considered the code-base "frozen". We did not make any adjustments to our system based on insights from the annotation or evaluation process until the evaluation was complete and all data was gathered. In contrast, we continually improved the zero-shot baseline approach during the evaluation process.

6.1 Zero-Shot Classification Baseline

For our zero-shot baseline we leverage the bart-large-mnli[18] checkpoint provided by Meta on Huggingface (Wolf et al., 2020). This zero-shot text classifier can take a label set and text as input and will return probability scores for the labels passed.

The model is based on a textual entailment framework which can work without annotated data of seen labels (Yin et al., 2019), an approach that has been adopted by previous work (such as Ye et al., 2020; Sainz and Rigau, 2021; Sun et al., 2021).

To recast our EE task as text classification, we provided the utterance as the text to be classified and the event labels as the classes. The labels provided were slightly adjusted to make them more amenable to the natural language expections of the approach (e.g., we changed "Move" to "movement" and "KnowledgeSharing" to "inform"). While we feel that the labels given to the zero-shot classifier could be further improved, we consider this to be beyond the scope of this work.

Since we require the classifier to be able to predict more than one event at a time, we cannot simply take an *argmax*. In an effort to more fairly compare the zero-shot model with our rule-based approach, we sampled different approaches for cut-off points of the label probability scores to serve as thresholds for extracting the events. Unfortunately, all methods sampled yielded overall micro F1 scores of < 0.1 (< 0.2 for macro F1) for the classifier.

While we believe it is likely that with further optimization we could have improved the performance of the zero-shot baseline, we hypothesize that the improvement would be limited. The data we are processing is real spoken language produced during times of stress and high focus for the participants. It is not comparable to the type of text-based data most modern large transformers are trained on.

However, we also implemented an oracle approach for the classifier that yielded much stronger performance. In our oracle approach, for each utterance we select the top n outputs of the zero-shot classifier as the given output, where n is the num-

[16] For example, a player might use the term "victim" multiple times in a single utterance.

[17] An implementation detail is that our system assigns a "GenericAction" label to events that it does not recognize. These event labels will only be exported by the system if they become an argument of a later event. When creating the dataset, if the arguments contained "GenericAction" events, we did not consider the event for annotation.

[18] `https://huggingface.co/facebook/bart-large-mnli`

	Event Label	Precision		Recall		F1		Support
		Rule-based	Zero-shot	Rule-based	Zero-shot	Rule-based	Zero-shot	
Simple	CriticalVictim	**0.959**	0.751	**0.729**	0.423	**0.828**	0.541	350
	Victim	**0.870**	0.691	**0.804**	0.561	**0.836**	0.619	342
	Room	**0.997**	0.572	**0.939**	0.286	**0.968**	0.381	809
	Engineer	**1.000**	0.957	**0.997**	0.609	**0.998**	0.744	294
	Transporter	**1.000**	0.303	**0.986**	0.888	**0.993**	0.451	277
	Medic	**1.000**	0.696	**1.000**	0.567	**1.000**	0.625	210
	Rubble	**1.000**	0.950	**0.986**	0.551	**0.993**	0.697	69
	MarkerBlock	**1.000**	0.272	**0.833**	0.708	**0.909**	0.393	48
	Meeting	**0.978**	0.279	**1.000**	0.856	**0.989**	0.421	90
	All simple (weighted av.)	**0.975**	0.634	**0.910**	0.508	**0.940**	0.518	2489
Complex	Move	**0.912**	0.254	**0.804**	0.595	**0.855**	0.356	296
	Precedence	**0.745**	0.112	**0.976**	0.159	**0.845**	0.132	126
	RescueInteractions	**0.792**	0.091	**0.528**	0.222	**0.633**	0.129	36
	KnowledgeSharing	**0.948**	0.246	**0.704**	0.111	**0.808**	0.154	314
	ReportLocation	**0.849**	0.127	**0.745**	0.236	**0.794**	0.165	106
	Search**	**0.818**	0.064	–	0.156	–	0.091	45
	HelpRequest	**0.805**	0.098	**0.713**	0.057	**0.756**	0.072	87
	Question	**0.705**	0.308	**0.298**	0.038	**0.419**	0.068	104
	YesNoQuestion	**0.827**	0.248	**0.684**	0.120	**0.749**	0.161	209
	Instruction	**0.700**	0.133	**0.531**	0.018	**0.604**	0.031	224
	Plan	**0.814**	0.645	**0.855**	0.045	**0.834**	0.084	447
	All complex (weighted av.)	**0.829**	0.299	**0.733**	0.165	**0.770**	0.144	1994
	All events (weighted av.)	**0.844**	0.528	**0.829**	0.472	**0.840**	0.450	4483

Table 1: Comparison of our rule-based EE system and the zero-shot baseline system for our coarse-grained evaluation. The zero-shot scores are all for the oracle setting, where we assume knowledge of the gold number of unique events in the utterance. The rule-based system does not use this oracle knowledge.

Event Label	Precision	Support
Move	0.942	120
Precedence	0.978	46
RescueInteractions	1.0	21
KnowledgeSharing	0.981	159
ReportLocation	1.0	57
Search	1.0	14
HelpRequest	0.961	26
Question	0.923	52
YesNoQuestion	1.0	21
Instruction	0.917	12
Plan	0.974	155
Weighted average	0.969	683

Table 2: Weighted average of argument structure precision scores for our rule-based approach (for events with arguments).

ber of unique gold labels for the utterance. While this method is not realistic, as it requires a-priori knowledge of the number of gold labels, it allowed us to generate a stronger baseline for comparison. Note we did *not* provide this knowledge to our rule-based approach.

7 Results

Table 1 shows the results of our evaluation. Our rule-based system achieves micro F1 scores of 0.940 and 0.770 for simple and complex events respectively.

The oracle zero-shot classifier baseline shows a micro F1 score of 0.518 for simple events and 0.144 for complex events. Our system outperforms the baseline on every event label, with the gap being particularly pronounced for domain-specific complex events such as "RescueInteractions".

In our system, both simple and complex events display consistently higher precision than recall, with "Precedence"[19] being the only exception. This outcome is expected; we designed the rules to favor precision over recall because the outputs of the EE system form inputs for further downstream tasks.

Table 2 shows the results for the precision-only fine-grained argument structure evaluation. Those events that can take arguments score a weighted average of 0.969 for precision of their argument structure.

[19]"Search" also displays higher recall than precision, but this is due to annotators not assigning any Search labels at all. We removed the recall score for the Search label from the table to reflect this fact.

8 Conclusion

Here we presented a case study on extracting team coordination events from natural language dialog. This dialog consists of live communications, which suffer from mistranscriptions, gap fillers, and interrupted or truncated utterances. While supervised neural approaches make up much of the recent literature for event extraction, these approaches become infeasible for this task due to the lack of training data. Further, the rapidly changing requirements for what should be extracted, as well as the need to embed domain-specific knowledge, led us to implement a rule-based approach.

Recently, large-scale pretrained language models have made zero shot and/or prompting-based approaches a convenient go-to for strong baselines, as these approaches make knowledge gained through large-scale pretraining accessible to various tasks. For this reason, we compare our rule-based method to a zero-shot classifier approach. We showed that in our case, our rule-based method out-performed the classifier for all event types we considered. Furthermore, the events output by our rules contain rich structure that can be used by downstream components for inference.

References

Wasi Uddin Ahmad, Nanyun Peng, and Kai-Wei Chang. 2021. GATE: Graph Attention Transformer Encoder for cross-lingual relation and event extraction. In *Thirty-Fifth AAAI Conference on Artificial Intelligence, AAAI 2021, Thirty-Third Conference on Innovative Applications of Artificial Intelligence, IAAI 2021, The Eleventh Symposium on Educational Advances in Artificial Intelligence, EAAI 2021, Virtual Event, February 2-9, 2021*, pages 12462–12470. AAAI Press.

Douglas E Appelt and Boyan Onyshkevych. 1998. The common pattern specification language. In *Proc. of the TIPSTER Workshop*, pages 23–30.

Laura Chiticariu, Yunyao Li, and Frederick R. Reiss. 2013. Rule-based information extraction is dead! Long live rule-based information extraction systems! In *Proceedings of the 2013 Conference on Empirical Methods in Natural Language Processing*, pages 827–832, Seattle, Washington, USA. Association for Computational Linguistics.

Hamish Cunningham, Diana Maynard, Kalina Bontcheva, and Valentin Tablan. 2002. Gate: an architecture for development of robust hlt applications. In *Proceedings of the 40th annual meeting on association for computational linguistics*, pages 168–175. Association for Computational Linguistics.

Xinya Du and Claire Cardie. 2020a. Event extraction by answering (almost) natural questions. In *Proceedings of the 2020 Conference on Empirical Methods in Natural Language Processing, EMNLP 2020, Online, November 16-20, 2020*, pages 671–683. Association for Computational Linguistics.

Xinya Du and Claire Cardie. 2020b. Event extraction by answering (almost) natural questions. *arXiv preprint arXiv:2004.13625*.

Lixiao Huang, Jared Freeman, Nancy Cooke, John Colonna-Romano, Matthew D Wood, Verica Buchanan, and Stephen J Caufman. 2022a. Exercises for artificial social intelligence in Minecraft search and rescue for teams.

Lixiao Huang, Jared Freeman, Nancy Cooke, John "JCR" Colonna-Romano, Matt Wood, Verica Buchanan, and Stephen Caufman. 2022b. Artificial Social Intelligence for Successful Teams (ASIST) Study 3.

Lawrence Hunter, Zhiyong Lu, James Firby, William A Baumgartner, Helen L Johnson, Philip V Ogren, and K Bretonnel Cohen. 2008. Opendmap: an open source, ontology-driven concept analysis engine, with applications to capturing knowledge regarding protein transport, protein interactions and cell-type-specific gene expression. *BMC bioinformatics*, 9(1):78.

Sarthak Jain and Byron C. Wallace. 2019. Attention is not Explanation. In *Proceedings of the 2019 Conference of the North American Chapter of the Association for Computational Linguistics: Human Language Technologies, Volume 1 (Long and Short Papers)*, pages 3543–3556, Minneapolis, Minnesota. Association for Computational Linguistics.

Roger Levy and Galen Andrew. 2006. Tregex and Tsurgeon: tools for querying and manipulating tree data structures. In *Proc. of LREC*.

Pengfei Liu, Weizhe Yuan, Jinlan Fu, Zhengbao Jiang, Hiroaki Hayashi, and Graham Neubig. 2021. Pretrain, prompt, and predict: A systematic survey of prompting methods in natural language processing. *arXiv preprint arXiv:2107.13586*.

Xiao Liu, Zhunchen Luo, and Heyan Huang. 2018. Jointly multiple events extraction via attention-based graph information aggregation. *arXiv preprint arXiv:1809.09078*.

Bonan Min, Hayley Ross, Elior Sulem, Amir Pouran Ben Veyseh, Thien Huu Nguyen, Oscar Sainz, Eneko Agirre, Ilana Heinz, and Dan Roth. 2021. Recent advances in natural language processing via large pre-trained language models: A survey. *arXiv preprint arXiv:2111.01243*.

Thien Huu Nguyen, Kyunghyun Cho, and Ralph Grishman. 2016a. Joint event extraction via recurrent neural networks. In *Proceedings of the 2016 Conference of the North American Chapter of the Association for Computational Linguistics: Human Language Technologies*, pages 300–309, San Diego, California. Association for Computational Linguistics.

Thien Huu Nguyen, Kyunghyun Cho, and Ralph Grishman. 2016b. Joint event extraction via recurrent neural networks. In *Proceedings of the 2016 Conference of the North American Chapter of the Association for Computational Linguistics: Human Language Technologies*, pages 300–309.

Trung Minh Nguyen and Thien Huu Nguyen. 2019. One for all: Neural joint modeling of entities and events. In *Proceedings of the AAAI conference on artificial intelligence*, volume 33, pages 6851–6858.

Adarsh Pyarelal. 2022. Tomcat (uaz + tamu) study 3 preregistration.

Oscar Sainz and German Rigau. 2021. Ask2transformers: Zero-shot domain labelling with pre-trained language models. *arXiv preprint arXiv:2101.02661*.

Lei Sha, Feng Qian, Baobao Chang, and Zhifang Sui. 2018. Jointly extracting event triggers and arguments by dependency-bridge rnn and tensor-based argument interaction. In *Proceedings of the AAAI conference on artificial intelligence*, volume 32.

Rebecca Sharp, Adarsh Pyarelal, Benjamin Gyori, Keith Alcock, Egoitz Laparra, Marco A. Valenzuela-Escárcega, Ajay Nagesh, Vikas Yadav, John Bachman, Zheng Tang, Heather Lent, Fan Luo, Mithun Paul, Steven Bethard, Kobus Barnard, Clayton Morrison, and Mihai Surdeanu. 2019. Eidos, INDRA, & Delphi: From free text to executable causal models. In *Proceedings of the 2019 Conference of the North American Chapter of the Association for Computational Linguistics (Demonstrations)*, pages 42–47, Minneapolis, Minnesota. Association for Computational Linguistics.

Yi Sun, Yu Zheng, Chao Hao, and Hangping Qiu. 2021. Nsp-bert: A prompt-based zero-shot learner through an original pre-training task–next sentence prediction. *arXiv preprint arXiv:2109.03564*.

Alex Tozzo, Dejan Jovanović, and Mohamed Amer. 2018. Neural event extraction from movies description. In *Proceedings of the First Workshop on Storytelling*, pages 60–66, New Orleans, Louisiana. Association for Computational Linguistics.

Marco A Valenzuela-Escárcega, Özgün Babur, Gus Hahn-Powell, Dane Bell, Thomas Hicks, Enrique Noriega-Atala, Xia Wang, Mihai Surdeanu, Emek Demir, and Clayton T Morrison. 2018. Large-scale automated machine reading discovers new cancer-driving mechanisms. *Database*, 2018.

Marco A. Valenzuela-Escárcega, Gus Hahn-Powell, and Mihai Surdeanu. 2016. Odin's runes: A rule language for information extraction. In *Proceedings of the Tenth International Conference on Language Resources and Evaluation (LREC'16)*, pages 322–329,

Portorož, Slovenia. European Language Resources Association (ELRA).

Marco A. Valenzuela-Escárcega, Gus Hahn-Powell, Mihai Surdeanu, and Thomas Hicks. 2015. A domain-independent rule-based framework for event extraction. In *Proceedings of ACL-IJCNLP 2015 System Demonstrations*, pages 127–132, Beijing, China. Association for Computational Linguistics and The Asian Federation of Natural Language Processing.

David Wadden, Ulme Wennberg, Yi Luan, and Hannaneh Hajishirzi. 2019. Entity, relation, and event extraction with contextualized span representations. *arXiv preprint arXiv:1909.03546*.

Jason Wei, Maarten Bosma, Vincent Y Zhao, Kelvin Guu, Adams Wei Yu, Brian Lester, Nan Du, Andrew M Dai, and Quoc V Le. 2021. Finetuned language models are zero-shot learners. *arXiv preprint arXiv:2109.01652*.

Thomas Wolf, Lysandre Debut, Victor Sanh, Julien Chaumond, Clement Delangue, Anthony Moi, Pierric Cistac, Tim Rault, Remi Louf, Morgan Funtowicz, Joe Davison, Sam Shleifer, Patrick von Platen, Clara Ma, Yacine Jernite, Julien Plu, Canwen Xu, Teven Le Scao, Sylvain Gugger, Mariama Drame, Quentin Lhoest, and Alexander Rush. 2020. Transformers: State-of-the-art natural language processing. In *Proceedings of the 2020 Conference on Empirical Methods in Natural Language Processing: System Demonstrations*, pages 38–45, Online. Association for Computational Linguistics.

Wei Xiang and Bang Wang. 2019. A survey of event extraction from text. *IEEE Access*, 7:173111–173137.

Zhiquan Ye, Yuxia Geng, Jiaoyan Chen, Jingmin Chen, Xiaoxiao Xu, Suhang Zheng, Feng Wang, Jun Zhang, and Huajun Chen. 2020. Zero-shot text classification via reinforced self-training. In *Proceedings of the 58th Annual Meeting of the Association for Computational Linguistics*, pages 3014–3024.

Wenpeng Yin, Jamaal Hay, and Dan Roth. 2019. Benchmarking zero-shot text classification: Datasets, evaluation and entailment approach. *arXiv preprint arXiv:1909.00161*.

Appendix

List of event labels and their meanings

What follows is a list of event labels we used for the evaluation. We provide explanations for each event and examples, some from the data used for this paper.

Simple Events

1. **CriticalVictim**: ASIST mission participants can encounter regular victims and critical victims. Critical victims require the entire team to save them. Examples: “type C”, “critical guy”, “c type”
2. **Victim**: Regular victims can be saved by the team member with the medic role. Examples: “guy in C3”, “type a person”, “b type victim”
3. **Room**: This is a collection of different room type events. We have specific event labels for every room on the map of any given experiment. Examples: “A2”, “room”, “office”
4. **Engineer**: One of the possible roles a player can assume. The engineer can clear rubble that is blocking the players’ path. Examples: “rubble guy”, “engineer”, “shovel guy”
5. **Transporter**: Assuming the transporter role allows players to move faster and to transport regular victims. Examples: “transporter”, “transport specialist”, “scout”
6. **Medic**: The medic can triage victims. Triaging victims yields points for the team. Examples: “medic”, “medical specialist”, “healer”
7. **Rubble**: Players will encounter rubble blocking their path on their mission. Examples: “gravel”, “rubble”, “rebel” (common mistranscription), “blockage”
8. **MarkerBlock**: Participants can drop a series of different markers on the floor. These can have different meanings and are used to mark important rooms etc. This event label is a collection of all specific marker block event labels. Examples: “c victim marker”, “gravel marker”, “victim block”, “threat sign”
9. **Meeting**: One of the participants will have a list of meetings that were going on when the building collapsed and their location. This is a collection of event labels capturing the terms used for those meetings. Examples: “management meeting”, “lunch”

Complex Events

10. **Move**: A collection of different event labels capturing participants discussing movement of themselves and others. Examples: “I’m on my way”, “Can you come to A2?”, “entering c1”

11. **Precedence**: A collection of different event labels capturing participants discussing temporal precedence. The event arguments aim to sort the two actions as an initial and subsequent action. Examples: "same thing M1 M1 M3 and then we can go i4a and then I2", "after I4 let's go to j4"

12. **RescueInteractions**: Participants can triage, wake up, and stabilize victims. This is a collection of labels capturing all these cases. Examples: "heading back to get all the victims", "yeah I can get this one let's wake up the there he's awake"

13. **KnowledgeSharing**: This event captures participants relaying information about entities that exist around them. Examples: "there's loads of victims in here", "there's a critical condition in the back"

14. **ReportLocation**: This event captures participants reporting their own location or the location of other entities. It also captures participants relaying certain information about the location.[20] Examples: "yeah I'm right I'm right by C6", "M3 is a trap room"

15. **Search**: This event captures participants talking about searching a room for victims. Examples: "we have searched F4 F4 is lunch this is medic", "have you checked a4a"

16. **HelpRequest**: Participants requesting help. This is a collection of different event labels which can be summarized under this umbrella. Examples: "if someone could help me I am trapped in j4", "and transporter if you can also assist in j4"

17. **Question**: Participants asking content questions. Examples: "this is the engineer how do you guys know whether they goes north or south"

18. **YesNoQuestion**: Participants asking binary questions. Examples: "do we clear this out"

19. **Instruction**: Participants giving instructions. Examples: "go to the middle section there's about 45 criticals so we know there's points there"

20. **Plan**: Participants engaging in planning. Examples: "okay if we want to start on i4a just to get some people moving", "okay I'll take care of the B type"

[20]This is handled by different event labels which are summarized under this event label for the purpose of the evaluation.

Listing 1: Example JSON output for "I'll head there first oh jeez what."


```
{
  "participant_id": "----",
  "asr_msg_id": "----",
  "text": "I'll head there first oh jeez what.",
  "utterance_source": {
    "source_type": "message_bus",
    "source_name": "agent/asr/final"
  },
  "extractions": [
  {
    "labels": [
    "DeliberatePlan",
    "Commitment",
    "Plan",
    "Communicate",
    "SimpleAction",
    "Action",
    "EventLike",
    "Concept"
    ],
    "span": "will head there",
    "arguments": {
      "topic": [
      {
        "labels": [
        "MoveTo",
        "Move",
        "SimpleAction",
        "Action",
        "EventLike",
        "Concept"
        ],
        "span": "head there",
        "arguments": {
          "target": [
          {
            "labels": [
            "Deictic",
            "Inferred",
            "Location",
            "EventLike",
            "Concept"
            ],
            "span": "there",
            "arguments": {},
            "attachments": [],
            "start_offset": 10,
            "end_offset": 15,
            "rule": "deictic_detection"
          }
          ]
        },
        "attachments": [
        {
          "text": "I",
          "agentType": "Self",
          "labels": [
          "Self",
          "Entity",
          "Concept"
          ],
          "span": [
          0
          ]
        },
        {
          "value": "future"
        }
        ],
        "start_offset": 5,
        "end_offset": 15,
        "rule": "move_deixis_action"
      }
      ]
    },
    "attachments": [
    {
      "text": "I",
      "agentType": "Self",
      "labels": [
      "Self",
      "Entity",
      "Concept"
      ],
      "span": [
      0
      ]
    },
    {
      "value": "future"
    }
    ],
    "start_offset": 1,
    "end_offset": 15,
    "rule": "commit_to_something_plan-type"
  },
  {
    "labels": [
    "MoveTo",
    "Move",
    "SimpleAction",
    "Action",
    "EventLike",
    "Concept"
    ],
    "span": "head there",
    "arguments": {
      "target": [
      {
        "labels": [
        "Deictic",
        "Inferred",
        "Location",
        "EventLike",
        "Concept"
        ],
        "span": "there",
        "arguments": {},
        "attachments": [],
        "start_offset": 10,
        "end_offset": 15,
        "rule": "deictic_detection"
      }
      ]
    },
    "attachments": [
    {
      "text": "I",
      "agentType": "Self",
      "labels": [
      "Self",
      "Entity",
      "Concept"
      ],
      "span": [
```

```
          0
          ]
        },
        {
          "value": "future"
        }
      ],
      "start_offset": 5,
      "end_offset": 15,
      "rule": "move_deixis_action"
    }
  ]
}
```


Listing 2: Sample of a subsection of the Label Ontology

```
- Communicate:
  - Instruction:
    - HelpCommand # for players instructing others to help, f.e.: "Help the engineer!"
  - ReportStatus:
    - Stuck # for players stuck in a room (for whichever reason), has some overlap with AmTrapped
    - ReportLocation # players reporting on their, or other players locations: "I'm in B2"
    - RoleDeclare # players declaring their role to the team
    - RoomStatus:
      - RoomClear # "A1 is clear"
      - ReportThreatRoom # players declaring rooms as threatrooms: "A1 is a threat room"
  - KnowledgeSharing # players reporting that something exists: "There is a critical victim here" or "I have some rubble in B2"
  - Need: # labels for players discussing the needs of the team or their own needs
    - NeedRole
    - NeedItem
    - NeedAction
```

Example Rule with Commentary

Listing 3: Example Rule

```
- name: "Help_command"
  label: HelpCommand
  example: "You should help him."
  priority: ${ rulepriority }
  pattern: |
  trigger = [lemma=/assist|help|aid|support/]
  agent: Entity = >nsubj [!mention=Self] |<xcomp >nsubj [!mention=Self]
  helpee: Entity = >ccomp >nsubj [!mention=You] | >ccomp [!mention=You] | >dep [!mention=You] | >dobj [!mention=You]
  location: Location? = >/${preps}/|
    >/advmod/
```

- `name`: Every Odin rule requires a unique name.
- `label`: This field defines the actual label that this rule will export. The label's place in the ontology is defined elsewhere

- example: We try and provide an example with each rule, for easier development.
- priority: This field defines at which iteration the rule will be applied. In this case this is defined via a vaiable.
- pattern: The pattern field defines the trigger and its arguments.
- trigger: Rules with an argument need a trigger field. If the trigger is found, the rule starts searching for the arguments. In this case, the trigger is defined as series of possible lemmas.
- agent: Entity – This field states that this rule takes an "agent" argument which as to carry the label "Entity" (or any of the subordinate labels of entity)
- >nsubj [!mention=Self] |<xcomp >nsubj [!mention=Self]: These statements define the *dependency relationship* that the agent argument needs to have with respect to the trigger. In plain English, this statement requires: An outgoing "nsubj" dependency, at the end of which there may **not** be an event label *You*, or an outgoing "ccomp" dependency, at the end of which there may **not** be an event label *You*, and so on.

Neural-Guided Program Synthesis of Information Extraction Rules Using Self-Supervision

Enrique Noriega-Atala[♠], Robert Vacareanu[♠,♣], Gustave Hahn-Powell[♠], and Marco Antonio Valenzuela-Escárcega

[♠]University of Arizona, Tucson, AZ, USA
[♣]Technical University of Cluj-Napoca, Cluj-Napoca, Romania
{enoriega,rvacareanu,hahnpowell}@arizona.edu
macrovalenzuelaescarcega@gmail.com

Abstract

In this work we propose a neural-based approach for rule synthesis designed to help bridge the gap between the interpretability, precision and maintainability exhibited by rule-based information extraction systems with the scalability and convenience of statistical information extraction systems. This is achieved by avoiding placing the burden of learning another specialized language on domain experts and instead asking them to provide a small set of examples in the form of highlighted spans of text. We introduce a transformer-based architecture that drives a rule synthesis system that leverages a self-supervised approach for pre-training a large-scale language model complemented by an analysis of different loss functions and aggregation mechanisms for variable length sequences of user-annotated spans of text. The results are encouraging and point to different desirable properties, such as speed and quality, depending on the choice of loss and aggregation method.

1 Introduction

Rule-based information extraction is interpretable, maintainable, and highly precise, but typically requires both domain expertise and deep knowledge of an esoteric rule language. The language barrier presents a major impediment to adoption for subject matter experts who are otherwise comfortable with providing examples of their information need in the form of a handful of highlighted spans of text. Synthesizing information extraction rules from such examples has the potential to bridge this divide and empower subject matter experts, but how can we learn to synthesize such programs for any domain? We propose a self-supervised approach for pre-training a large-scale language model for synthesizing information extraction rules using randomly generated rules (programs) paired with matched spans in context (program specifications). The contributions of this work are:

- A transformer-based neural architecture for rule scoring designed to drive a rule synthesis process by jointly encoding candidate rules and a specification that represents the user's intent.
- The introduction of a relevant in domain self-supervised pre-training objective for the rule synthesis problem.
- The exploration of different training scenarios using different loss functions and aggregation methods to score candidate rules in the presence of variable length user specifications.

2 Related Work

Generating computer programs automatically has been a longstanding dream within the field of Artificial Intelligence. The goal of program synthesis is to generate programs from a high-level *specification*[1] (Gulwani et al., 2017). Existing approaches to program synthesis fall into one of two broad categories: search-based methods (e.g., enumerative search, stochastic search (Alur et al., 2013) etc.) and constraint satisfaction (Solar-Lezama, 2009; Torlak and Bodik, 2013). In this work, we focus on search-based program synthesis (Alur et al., 2018), specifically a neural-guided enumerative search.

Neural approaches have come to dominate search-based program synthesis (Balog et al., 2016; Parisotto et al., 2016; Kalyan et al., 2018). Similar to Parisotto et al. (2016), our approach learns a distribution over programs to guide every step of the search. Unlike Parisotto et al. (2016), however, we score only the transitions allowed by the DSL grammar and encode the specification in a manner which reflects that our programs are meant to match natural language.

Rule-based information extraction systems are more interpretable than its statistical counterparts.

[1]A description (visual, example-based, etc.) of what the program should accomplish.

Proceedings of the 29th International Conference on Computational Linguistic, pages 85–93
October 12–17, 2022.

Rule languages with high expressiveness allow to model complex surface and syntactic patterns (Valenzuela-Escárcega et al., 2016). These systems are suitable to create highly specialized domain-specific information extraction tools without the need of large and expensive annotated datasets (Valenzuela-Escárcega et al., 2018). Unfortunately, mastering rule-based systems often implies a steep learning curve and a significant time investment by domain experts.

In this work we focus on the intersection of both pattern-based and neural-based techniques by training a statistical model to *synthesize* rule patterns by exposing it to user-provided examples.

3 Odinson Information Extraction System

In this work, we are interested in synthesizing information extraction rules expressed in a domain specific language (DSL) first described in Valenzuela-Escárcega et al. (2016). This language supports extraction rules based on token constraints (e.g., parts-of-speech and lemmas) as well as syntactic patterns. However, only surface rules are targeted in this work, leaving support for syntactic rules for future work.

We apply the rules expressed in the DSL using the Odinson information extraction framework (Valenzuela-Escárcega et al., 2020), which supports the efficient application of the extraction rules over a large corpus through the use of a custom Lucene[2] index. Like Lucene, Odinson can store an index on-disk or in-memory, and we take advantage of both indexes types during this work. An on-disk index is used to store a large corpus used during the data generation process described in Section 5, and an in-memory index is created on-the-fly during the enumerative search to store the sentences that form part of the user *specification*, indicated in Algorithm 1 as the $make\_index()$ function.

4 Enumerative Search

The enumerative search procedure, outlined in Algorithm 1, takes as input a *user specification*, (referred to as specification for brevity) comprised of a collection of sentences and a set of spans representing the desired extractions; a *rule scorer* component which drives the behavior of the search; and a *performance threshold* that functions as a stopping criteria for the search.

The specification encodes the user's intent and is the main source of signal at the time of scoring any given partial rule encountered during the search.

Rules are composed of syntactic elements defined by the DSL. One noteworthy element is the *placeholder*, represented by the symbol □, which is introduced to represent an underspecified portion of the rule that must be expanded by following the grammar of the DSL. A rule is considered *valid* (grammatical) if it has no placeholders, otherwise it is a *partial* rule containing one or more placeholder. Partial rules are subject to further expansions of the form allowed by the DSL grammar.

To conduct an enumerative search, we create an in-memory index containing the phrases included in the rule's specification and initialize a priority queue with a partial rule consisting of a single placeholder (i.e., the root of the search tree). At each iteration, we retrieve the top-ranked partial rule in the priority queue and check its validity. If it is a valid rule, we query the index to verify if the rule matches the spans highlighted in the specification, and compute a score to measure the rule's performance (e.g., an F1 score over the spans matched in the specification). If the score is above some threshold[3], the candidate rule is returned. If the rule still contains placeholders, we expand the left-most placeholder according to our DSL grammar and use the rule scorer to produce a score for each of the expanded rules with respect to the user-provided specification. Each expanded rule is placed into the priority queue according to its score. The process repeats until a complete rule is found that meets or exceeds the specified performance threshold.

Our enumerative search process implements the branch-and-bound algorithm (Land and Doig, 1960) using a priority queue. An ideal scorer would guide the expansions directly to a correct rule approximating a depth-first search, but the priority queue allows the search to *backtrack* to the most promising candidate if necessary.

It is worth noting that the rule scorer component of the algorithm can be any function that takes as input a partial rule and the specification, and returns a score denoting the rule's priority for further expansion. In the remaining sections of this work, we describe neural architectures for training rule

[2]`https://lucene.apache.org/`

[3]A system hyperparameter.

scoring models (§7.1) with supervised training data (§5).

Algorithm 1 Enumerative search.

```
Require: spec                          ▷ user specification
Require: scorer                        ▷ partial rule scorer
Require: threshold                     ▷ score threshold
  (sentences, gold_spans) ← spec
  index ← make_index(sentences)
  queue ← priority_queue()
  push(queue, □, ∞)
  while queue ≠ ∅ do
      candidate ← pop(queue)
      if is_valid(candidate) then
          results ← query(index, candidate)
          score ← eval(results, gold_spans)
          if score ≥ threshold then
              return candidate
          end if
      else
          children ← expand(candidate)
          for all child ∈ children do
              score ← scorer(child, spec)
              push(queue, child, score)
          end for
      end if
  end while
```

5 Data Generation

To learn to synthesize information extraction rules in a supervised fashion, we first need $(spec, rule)$ pairs. Conceptually, a *spec* (i.e., matches in context) is easily obtained by querying an index, as long as the $rule$ is available. Our data generation pipeline can be broken down into 4 steps, as highlighted in Algorithm 2.

Algorithm 2 The algorithm to generate $(spec, rule)$ pairs without any supervision

1: Generate a random rule r
2: Query the index using the rule r
3: Select a spec s out of all the query results
4: Return (s, r)

In order to generate a rule (step 1 in Algorithm 2), we need a sentence and a span of interest.[4]

[4]In practice, this would be provided by a user (e.g., a domain expert). To generate data for our pre-training task in this work, we simply select a random sentence together with a random span within that sentence.

Then, we randomly manipulate constraints to alter the rule's complexity. After each subsequent change in the candidate rule, we query a large index to avoid generating rules without any matches. Once we have a final form of a rule, we use it to query the index and collect the matches (spans in context) to use as the rule's specification (*spec*). We describe our rule generation process in Algorithm 3.

Algorithm 3 The algorithm to generate a random rule

```
Require: Sentence sent together with span, a
    span inside sent
  rule ← surface_constraints(sent, span)
  rule ← random_constraints(rule)
  rule ← random_surface(rule)
```

The heart of our rule generation algorithm lies inside 3 functions: `surface_constraints`, `random_constraints`, and `random_surface`. Concretely, `surface_constraints` uses the underlying *tag, lemma,* or *word* constraints to generate an initial rule. Then, `random_constraints` adds additional token-level constraints, such as `and`, `or`, and `not`. Lastly, `random_surface` adds surface level constraints, such as wildcards and `or` constraints. For example, consider `The quick brown fox jumps over the lazy dog` together with the desired span *quick brown fox*. The `surface_constraints` will generate an initial rule, such as `[lemma=quick] [tag=JJ] [word=fox]`. Then, `random_constraints` will modify this initial rule and add random constraints, changing the rule to something like `[lemma=quick | lemma=fast] [tag=JJ] [word=fox]`. Then, `random_surface` adds surface level constraints. For example, the rule can now become `([lemma=quick | lemma=fast])? ([tag=JJ] | [word=lazy]) ([word=fox] | [word=cat])`. Note that both `random_constraints` and `random_surface` add a random number of changes to the initial rule.

6 Pre-training

We take inspiration from the Question-Answering community (Rajpurkar et al., 2016, 2018) and train a model to predict the span matched by a given rule in a given sentence. Concretely, we use a dataset generated according to the description in Section 5 and interpret the concatenation of the rule ($rule$) with the sentence ($sent$) as the question. Then, the self-supervised task becomes to predict the start and the end of the span, as in classical span-based question answering.

This pre-training objective has two aims. First, we expose the backbone model (a transformer) to the in-domain vocabulary in which the words and symbols of the DSL are much more frequent than they are in the Wikipedia or Book corpora (Devlin et al., 2019). Our second aim is to expose the model to an unfamiliar task closely related to our ultimate goal: span prediction (i.e., the match for an information extraction rule against some sentence). By learning to predict spans, the model is primed to learn to score candidate rules generated through enumerative search.

7 Rule Scorer Architecture

The heart of the enumerative search process lies at the *rule scoring function*. The rule scoring function assigns a priority value to each of the rule's expansions encountered throughout an enumerative search. Since priority scores control the exploration behavior during the search, it is critical to have an optimized scoring model that can discriminate between promising or futile rule expansions.

We opt to follow a data-driven approach to train a rule-scoring artificial neural network. Figure 1 depicts the architecture of scoring network. The network takes as input a rule: either partially or totally expanded, and the specification; as output, it produces a score used to prioritize a candidate rule in the search process.

We used the rule-specs described in §5 to build a dataset of transitions for rule scoring. We split the rules into training, development and testing with 1.5 million, 6,000 and 500 items, respectively. For the training and development subsets, we used the Odinson's language grammar to enumerate all the transitions necessary to derive each of the rules, and collected the transitions along the path from the root placeholder to the ground truth rule that matches the specification. To obtain negative examples, at any given step we collected the syntactically valid expansions that *don't lead* to the ground truth rule. Figure 2 shows an example of the expansion steps to generate a simple rule composes of two token constrains in DSL. Each row shows a transition, considered a positive training example while the rest of the other syntactically valid transitions (not shown in the figure) are used as negative examples.

Following this approach, the dataset contains 9,731,804 and 748,836 transitions in the training and development subsets, respectively. The ratio of positive to negative transitions is 1 to 3.21.

7.1 Encoding the Rule with the Specification

The provided specification encodes the intent of the rule. Without a specification, it is impossible to know what a rule is expected to match. In other words, the specification sets the context of a rule, and without it, there is no signal to guide the search process beyond the syntactic properties of the DSL's grammar and the statistics of the training dataset.

The specification consists of a variable length list of sentences with an annotated span that the target rule is expected to match. We propose a two-step method to encode a rule with its specification into a combined representation inspired in the investigation of different aggregation methods for multiple input sequences proposed by (Noriega-Atala et al., 2022). This rule-spec embedding is then used to compute the priority score.

In the first step, a partially expanded rule will be paired with each phrase in the spec. The pair is encoded by prepending the rule to the phrase, separated by the `[SEP]` token. Special markup tokens are inserted at the boundaries of the match. This annotated input sequence is then passed to a BERT-based encoder to generate a contextualized representation of the rule with one of its individual spec phrases. Figure 3 shows an example

In the second step, we aim to reduce all the contextualized representations of the partial rule to represent the totality of the user's intent into a fixed-size embedding. We achieve this by collecting the `[CLS]` tokens of the contextualized sequences from the previous step and aggregate them together using one of the following methods: *average*, *max-pooling over time* or an *attention mechanism* (Yang et al., 2016), whose attention matrix and single query vector are tunable parameters optimized during training.

8 Experiments

We tested the rule scoring architecture on several rule synthesis processes. For each model, we control the loss function (§8.1) used for training and

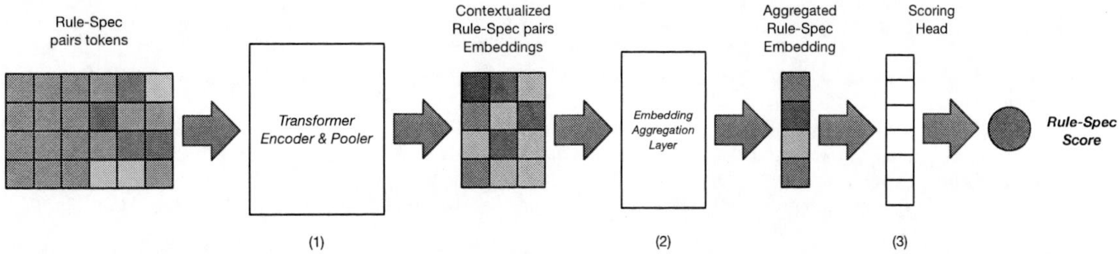

Figure 1: Rule scoring architecture. Step 1 takes as input the pair-wise concatenation of a) the partial rule and b) the annotated phrases in the provided specification. The input is fed through a foundation transformer model which outputs the `[CLS]` embedding for each rule-spec pair. Step 2 aggregates the matrix of `[CLS]` embeddings, either through average pooling or an attention layer, and outputs a fixed-size rule-spec vector. Step 3 linearly maps the rule-spec vector into a real-valued scalar score. The output score will be used as the priority value during the enumerative search process.

□ → □□
□□ ⟶ [□] □
[□] □ ⟶ [tag = □] □
[tag = □] □ ⟶ [tag = *JJ*] □
[tag = *JJ*] □ ⟶ [tag = *JJ*] [□]
[tag = *JJ*] [□] ⟶ [tag = *JJ*] [word = □]
[tag = *JJ*] [word = □] → [tag = *JJ*] [word = *rule*]

Figure 2: Expansion transitions to generate a rule. The transitions shown here are used as positive examples in the training set for the rule scoring model.

the method for aggregating the specification (§7.1). All models are fine-tuned on top of a BERT checkpoint pre-trained for rule span prediction (§6).

Each trained model was applied on a held-out test set of 500 rule synthesis problems with their respective specification. Each synthesis process was carried out by an enumerative search with a limit of 500 steps.

8.1 Loss Functions for Rule Scoring

One crucial property required to carry out enumerative search efficiently is the rule scoring function. The function must give a high score to rules generated from transitions leading towards a rule that matches the specification and vice-versa.

We explore two loss functions designed to reward accurate transitions and penalize transitions that don't lead towards the ground-truth rule.

8.2 MSE Loss

We use the mean squared error loss function (Equation 1) in which an expansion is scored as $i_i = 1$ when it the expansion is the result of a transition towards the ground-truth rule, and $l_i = 0$ otherwise. This loss configuration does not take into account any information about the location of the expansion in the AST of the rule.

$$\ell(\mathbf{l}, \mathbf{s}) = \frac{1}{n} \sum_{i=1}^{n} (l_i - s_i)^2 \tag{1}$$

8.3 Margin loss

Additionally, we use a margin loss function to train a scoring function to rank the scores of a rule with respect to the score of its parent. The element-wise loss function from Equation 2 takes as as input arguments two scores: A partial rule's score (s_c) and its parent's rule score (s_p). Each score is generated by a forward pass through the model. Individual losses within a batch are averaged to generate the batch's loss. Optimizing this loss will tune the model such that the difference between the pair of scores is at least as large as the margin hyperparameter m. This loss function is designed to give a higher score to a rule or partial rule than its parent if it was a transition leading towards the ground-truth and vice-versa. Ideally, this property should prioritize partial rules that are closer to matching the specification.

$$\ell(s_p, s_c, m) = \begin{cases} \max(0, m - s_c + s_p) \\ \quad \text{if } s_c \text{ is correct} \\ \max(0, m - s_p + s_c) \\ \quad \text{if } s_c \text{ is incorrect} \end{cases} \tag{2}$$

9 Results

Table 1 shows the number of problems for which each rule scoring model matched the user specification. Cases in which all the spans in the specification are matched exactly are considered *exact matches* and those where a span is missing or an incorrect span is matched are considered *partial*

`[CLS]` [tag = *JJR*] [lemma = *natural*] [□|□|□] □ `[SEP]` The **<MATCH>** more natural , or background **</MATCH>** , sound you can tape , the better . `[SEP]`

`[CLS]` [tag = *JJR*] [lemma = *natural*] [□|□|□] □ `[SEP]` so there are **<MATCH>** less natural , wild **</MATCH>**, hatchery fish that make it to the ocean `[SEP]`

`[CLS]` [tag = *JJR*] [lemma = *natural*] [□|□|□] □ `[SEP]` The further back one traces the race , the fewer are concerned in the government ; the fewer are so concerned , the **<MATCH>** more natural , **</MATCH>** because the easiest , is the system of effecting changes - aye , improvements - by " despatching " the government . `[SEP]`

Figure 3: Partial rule and its target specification encoded as input to a rule scoring network. The partial rule is paired with every phrase in the specification to attend to every match with a transformer encoder.The boundaries of the specification's spans are delimited with specially designated markup tokens in the architecture's tokenizer model. For each input sequence, the rule scoring network will pool the `[CLS]` output embedding as the contextualized representation of the partial rule with respect to its corresponding matching span. The matrix of `[CLS]` embeddings will reduced to fixed size rule-spec encoding with an aggregation layer as described in §7.1. The contents of this figure represent the left-most input block in figure 1

Loss Function	***Spec Aggregation***	*Exact Matches*	*Partial Matches*	*Any Matches*
Margin	Attention	68(14%)	263(53%)	331(67%)
Margin	Average	57(11%)	248(50%)	181(61%)
MSE	Attention	**113(23%)**	358(72%)	**471(95%)**
MSE	Average	84(17%)	**383(77%)**	838(94%)
Margin	No Spec	0	28(6%)	28(6%)

Table 1: Number of matches in the specifications of the testing set. Exact matches are cases in which all the spans in the specification are matched exactly. Partial matches are cases where a) a span is missing or b) an incorrect span is matched. Total matches are the sum of both.

matches. The right-most column counts the number of matches, irrespective of the type.

The architectures that aggregate the rule-span pair encodings using an attention mechanism are better at matching the specification in terms of exact and partial matches. Specifically, the model trained using the MSE loss function has the highest exact match rate and combined match rate. For any given problem, every span in the specification represents constraints for rule synthesis. These constraints interact together to encode some intent. We hypothesise that the attention mechanism helps capture the signal in those implicit constraint interactions better than averaging the rule-span pair encodings, which effectively weights the contribution of every encoding to the rule's score equally.

To highlight the crucial role of the specification, we trained a model that generates scores by only encoding partial rules, ignoring the specification during the enumerative search algorithm. This model is represented by the bottom row of the table. Its unsurprisingly poor performance illustrate how without the specification (which represents the intent), there is simply not enough signal to successfully synthesize a rule.

In addition to the number of matches of each model, we are also interested in the quality of the matches. Tables 2 and 3 show the macro and micro average performances of the rule scoring models, respectively. To compute precision, recall and F1 scores, a) matches to specification spans, b) matches to spans not in the specification, and c) unmatched spans in the specification are considered a) true positives, b) false positives, and c) and false negatives, respectively. The models that encode the rule and specification with attention outperform those that average. The attention mechanism also improves recall. These results are consonant with our hypothesis about the utility of the attention mechanism to model the interaction of the elements in the specification. In addition, models trained with the margin loss function are faster at synthesizing rules (i.e., they require fewer steps to generate a complete rule). This observation reflects the design, as the margin loss prioritizes partial rules close to complete expansion, resembling more a depth-first search approach, whereas training with MSE just estimates how "right" or

Loss Function	*Spec Aggregation*	*Precision*	*Recall*	*F1*	*Steps*
Margin	Attention	0.55 ± 0.02	0.34 ± 0.02	0.36 ± 0.02	$\mathbf{13.08 \pm 0.37}$
Margin	Average	0.49 ± 0.02	0.32 ± 0.02	0.33 ± 0.02	13.43 ± 0.46
MSE	Attention	$\mathbf{0.82 \pm 0.01}$	$\mathbf{0.50 \pm 0.02}$	$\mathbf{0.56 \pm 0.02}$	74.15 ± 3.65
MSE	Average	0.73 ± 0.02	0.45 ± 0.02	0.48 ± 0.01	55.55 ± 3.73
Margin	No Spec	0.01 ± 0.00	0.02 ± 0.01	0.01 ± 0.00	4.0 ± 0.0

Table 2: Macro-average performance of different rule scoring models on the testing set. Results are computed by evaluating the rules generated using enumerative search on their corresponding specification in the testing set (see §7). The testing dataset is bootstrapped re-sampled 10,000 times to calculate standard deviations of each metric. To compute precision, recall and F1 scores, a) matches to specification spans, b) matches to spans not in the specification, and c) unmatched spans in the specification are considered a) true positives, b) false positives, and c) false negatives, respectively. The steps column reports the average number of steps to successfully find a rule.

Loss Function	*Spec Aggregation*	*Precision*	*Recall*	*F1*
Margin	Attention	0.55 ± 0.03	$\mathbf{0.41 \pm 0.03}$	$\mathbf{0.47 \pm 0.02}$
Margin	Average	0.53 ± 0.03	$\mathbf{0.41 \pm 0.03}$	0.46 ± 0.03
MSE	Attention	$\mathbf{0.69 \pm 0.04}$	0.30 ± 0.02	0.42 ± 0.03
MSE	Average	0.32 ± 0.02	0.27 ± 0.02	0.30 ± 0.01
Margin	No Spec	0.13 ± 0.03	0.16 ± 0.04	0.14 ± 0.03

Table 3: Micro-average performance of different rule scoring models on the testing set. Results are computed by evaluating the rules generated using enumerative search on their corresponding specification in the testing set (see §7) and the matches to calculate micro average performance metrics. The testing dataset is bootstrapped re-sampled 10,000 times to calculate standard deviations of each metric. Metrics are compared similarly. The definitions of precision, recall and F1 are the same of table 2

"wrong" is the rule, and has no implicit consideration about how far or close a partial rule is to completing expansion.

We looked at the rules generated using the MSE+Attention rule-scoring model. Out of all the rules generated, approximately 2.5% perfectly match the gold rule. Nevertheless, approximately 20% of the generated rules obtain a perfect F1 score (i.e. 1.0). This is an example of *program aliasing*, where a different program produces the same result. In our case specifically, a different rule matches the same specification. We can observe this phenomenon in the first two rows of table 4. Nonetheless, there is still ample room for improvement, as we can see how sometimes the synthesizer generates a rule that misses most of the specification.

10 Future Work

The results presented in this work are promising and open the door for further research in several directions that will help to better understand the properties of the rule scoring architectures. In its current state, our approach has at least avenues to future work.

Extrinsic Analysis We evaluated the methods on a testing dataset. This evaluation is useful to compare the relative performance of the different architectures analyzed in this work. It is necessary to implement named captures to be able perform an *extrinsic* evaluation, similar to the evaluation protocol proposed by (Vacareanu et al., 2022) on an external dataset to validate the utility of our method for the information extraction task.

Finding equivalent rules Our training procedure prunes branches that will not lead to the target rule, but this may inadvertently prune paths leading to equivalent rules that match the same specification. The large search space makes it impractical to enumerate all equivalent rules for each specification. Reinforcement learning is a viable alternative to training a rule scoring model. Multiple rules that

Target Rule	*Synthesized Rule*	*F1*
`[tag=NN] [lemma=in] [raw=many] [word=of] [tag=PRP$]`	`[tag=NN] [lemma=in] [lemma=many] [lemma=of] [tag=PRP$]`	1.0
`[raw=always] [lemma=make] [tag=NNS] [word=that]`	`[lemma=alway] [tag=VBP] [lemma=decision] [lemma=that]`	1.0
`[lemma=describe] [raw=how] [word=the]`	`[tag=VBZ] [lemma=how] [tag=DT]`	0.59
`[lemma=mikhail | tag=NN]`	`[word=The | lemma=range]`	0.08

Table 4: Examples of rules generated with an enumerative search. Target Rule is the ground truth rule which matches the user specification. Synthesized Rule is the rule generated by the enumerative search process; F1 is the synthesized rule's score over the user specification for the corresponding target rule.

match the specification can be found by exploring the space of syntactically correct expansions. This could improve the expressiveness of a rule synthesis system and increase data efficiency without incorrectly penalizing valid rules that are not part of the training dataset in supervised learning.

Grammar synthesis The current approach assumes a single rule must match the entire specification. For diverse specifications (i.e., spans with highly varied contexts), a single rule may end up containing many disjunctive clauses. Long, complex rules may adversely affect interpretability and maintainability. Rather than generating a single rule for a specification, it may be advantageous in some cases to learn to generate a set of two or more complementary rules with low complexity and better generalization.

Interactive use The model trained using margin loss and an attention mechanism for encoding is able to find a rule much faster (on average) than the rest of the models without suffering a steep loss in performance. Further investigation is needed to understand not only what changes might increase the quality of the matches in rule synthesis but also what changes will make they system fast enough for interactive use.

References

Rajeev Alur, Rastislav Bodik, Garvit Juniwal, Milo M. K. Martin, Mukund Raghothaman, Sanjit A. Seshia, Rishabh Singh, Armando Solar-Lezama, Emina Torlak, and Abhishek Udupa. 2013. Syntax-guided synthesis. In *Formal Methods in Computer-Aided Design*, pages 1–8.

Rajeev Alur, Rishabh Singh, Dana Fisman, and Armando Solar-Lezama. 2018. Search-based program synthesis. *Communications of the ACM*, 61(12):84–93.

Matej Balog, Alexander L Gaunt, Marc Brockschmidt, Sebastian Nowozin, and Daniel Tarlow. 2016. Deepcoder: Learning to write programs. *arXiv preprint arXiv:1611.01989*.

Jacob Devlin, Ming-Wei Chang, Kenton Lee, and Kristina Toutanova. 2019. BERT: Pre-training of deep bidirectional transformers for language understanding. In *Proceedings of the 2019 Conference of the North American Chapter of the Association for Computational Linguistics: Human Language Technologies, Volume 1 (Long and Short Papers)*, pages 4171–4186, Minneapolis, Minnesota. Association for Computational Linguistics.

Sumit Gulwani, Oleksandr Polozov, Rishabh Singh, et al. 2017. Program synthesis. *Foundations and Trends® in Programming Languages*, 4(1-2):1–119.

Ashwin Kalyan, Abhishek Mohta, Oleksandr Polozov, Dhruv Batra, Prateek Jain, and Sumit Gulwani. 2018. Neural-guided deductive search for real-time program synthesis from examples. *arXiv preprint arXiv:1804.01186*.

AH Land and AG Doig. 1960. An automatic method of solving discrete programming problems. *Econometrica: Journal of the Econometric Society*, pages 497–520.

Enrique Noriega-Atala, Peter M. Lovett, Clayton Morrison, and Mihai Surdeanu. 2022. Neural architectures for biological inter-sentence relation extraction. In *Scientific Document Understanding 2022*, number 3164 in CEUR Workshop Proceedings.

Emilio Parisotto, Abdel-rahman Mohamed, Rishabh Singh, Lihong Li, Dengyong Zhou, and Pushmeet Kohli. 2016. Neuro-symbolic program synthesis. *arXiv preprint arXiv:1611.01855*.

Pranav Rajpurkar, Robin Jia, and Percy Liang. 2018. Know what you don't know: Unanswerable questions for squad. In *ACL*.

Pranav Rajpurkar, Jian Zhang, Konstantin Lopyrev, and Percy Liang. 2016. Squad: 100,000+ questions for machine comprehension of text. In *EMNLP*.

Armando Solar-Lezama. 2009. The sketching approach to program synthesis. In *Asian Symposium on Programming Languages and Systems*, pages 4–13. Springer.

Emina Torlak and Rastislav Bodik. 2013. Growing solver-aided languages with rosette. In *Proceedings of the 2013 ACM international symposium on New ideas, new paradigms, and reflections on programming & software*, pages 135–152.

Robert Vacareanu, Marco A. Valenzuela-Escárcega, George Barbosa, Rebecca Sharp, and Mihai Surdeanu. 2022. From examples to rules: Neural guided rule synthesis for information extraction. In *Proceedings of the 13th Language Resources and Evaluation Conference (LREC)*.

Marco A. Valenzuela-Escárcega, Gus Hahn-Powell, and Dane Bell. 2020. Odinson: A fast rule-based information extraction framework. In *Proceedings of the 12th Language Resources and Evaluation Conference*, pages 2183–2191, Marseille, France. European Language Resources Association.

Marco A. Valenzuela-Escárcega, Gus Hahn-Powell, and Mihai Surdeanu. 2016. Odin's runes: A rule language for information extraction. In *Proceedings of the Tenth International Conference on Language Resources and Evaluation (LREC'16)*, pages 322–329, Portorož, Slovenia. European Language Resources Association (ELRA).

Marco A Valenzuela-Escárcega, Özgün Babur, Gus Hahn-Powell, Dane Bell, Thomas Hicks, Enrique Noriega-Atala, Xia Wang, Mihai Surdeanu, Emek Demir, and Clayton T Morrison. 2018. Large-scale automated machine reading discovers new cancer-driving mechanisms. *Database*, 2018. Bay098.

Zichao Yang, Diyi Yang, Chris Dyer, Xiaodong He, Alex Smola, and Eduard Hovy. 2016. Hierarchical attention networks for document classification. In *Proceedings of the 2016 Conference of the North American Chapter of the Association for Computational Linguistics: Human Language Technologies*, pages 1480–1489, San Diego, California. Association for Computational Linguistics.

Author Index

Association for Computational Linguistics
209 N. Eighth Street
Stroudsburg, Pennsylvania 18360

ISBN 978-1-7138-6193-5

CURRAN ASSOCIATES INC.
proceedings.com